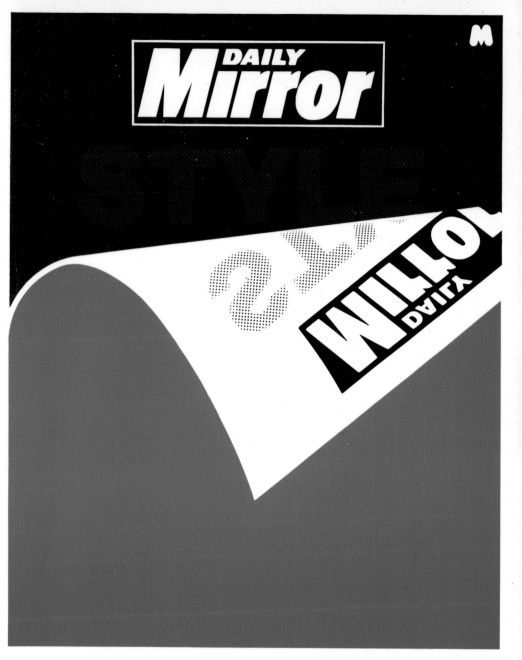

The Mirror's Way with Words
by
Keith Waterhouse

Daily Mirror style

It is clear that the decline of a language must ultimately have political and economic causes: it is not due simply to the bad influence of this or that individual writer. But an effect can become a cause, reinforcing the original cause and producing the same effect in an intensified form, and so on indefinitely. A man may take to drink because he feels himself to be a failure, and then fail all the more completely because he drinks. It is rather the same thing that is happening to the English language. It becomes ugly and inaccurate because our thoughts are foolish, but the slovenliness of our language makes it easier for us to have foolish thoughts.

George Orwell
Politics and the English Language

Daily Mirror style

Keith Waterhouse

MIRROR BOOKS

Grateful acknowledgement is made to the following newspapers for quotations used in this book: Daily Express, Daily Mail, Daily Star, The Daily Telegraph, Evening News, The Guardian, The Observer, The Sun.

Grateful thanks is made to Mrs Sonia Brownell Orwell for permission to quote from George Orwell's Politics and the English Language, first published in 1946. Now reissued in Collected Essays, Journalism and Letters, Martin Secker & Warburg Ltd, 1968.

First published in March 1981 in Great Britain by
Mirror Books Ltd., Athene House,
66/73 Shoe Lane, London EC4P 4AB
for Mirror Group Newspapers Ltd.
Printed and bound in Great Britain by
Main Printers Ltd., Mitcham, Surrey

ISBN 0 85939 246 5

Introduction

In most newspaper offices there is to be found a manual known as a style-book which lays down, for the sake of consistency, the paper's rules on the usage of words and punctuation. Thus do newcomers to The Times, for example, learn that in Printing House Square the spelling of *recognise* is *recognize*.

This is not a style-book in that sense. It is a book about the style of English used by newspapers, particularly popular newspapers.

Daily Mirror Style evolved from sporadic conversations over a period of months, indeed years, between the Editor of the Daily Mirror, Michael Molloy, the Chairman and Editorial Director of Mirror Group Newspapers, Anthony Miles, and myself, about the way the popular papers' use of language was developing. Finally I was asked if I would marshal some of these thoughts on paper, and so I went away and prepared this manual, drawing my examples of newspaper English mainly from stories that were being published as I was compiling it, in the summer of 1979. It was privately published for the Daily Mirror towards the end of that year.

It was gratifyingly well-received, even by senior old hands whose response might understandably have been that they didn't need lessons on how to suck eggs. Newcomers to our craft welcomed it as (so they told me) a rather more entertaining instruction manual than usually comes their way. Journalists on other newspapers begged copies for amusement rather than enlightenment. Finally, when continued demand for the book had outstripped supplies, it was decided to "go public" with a new edition.

I hope this edition will be read not only by journalists and students of journalism but by all sorts and manner of people with an interest in writing good plain English. It doesn't pretend to be a textbook, although you will find in it a few tips on avoiding grammatical pitfalls. What it is, if you like, is a polemic against shoddy or tired writing and a plea for fresh and workmanlike writing.

Apart from the addition of this introduction and the glossary of some of the peculiar printers' and journalists' terms that have found their way into its pages, this edition of *Daily Mirror Style* is exactly, in content, as it was originally published for private circulation within the Daily Mirror office. Since the Mirror is not let off lightly in my continuing examination of clichés, horrible puns, facetious wordplay and other excesses, it might be thought that a little prudent editing would have been in order. But that is not the Mirror's way. The paper that has Fleet Street's longest and most courageous record of dishing it out is also big enough to take it.

I have not adapted or modified the book for the general reader. I thought that if I did it would lose that peculiarly inky flavour of the bustling newspaper office in which it was compiled. Besides, I do believe that as it stands, *Daily Mirror Style* gives an interesting little glimpse behind the scenes, which would have been lost had I generalised its shoptalk element out of existence.

K.W.

Glossary

for non-journalists

BILLBOARD. A display typeface of the kind once used on theatre and circus posters.

BLURB. An announcement, usually lavish in nature, of what is in store for the reader.

BODY-TYPE. The main typeface in which an article is set.

BOLD (or Boldface). Thick black type used for emphasis.

BROADSHEET. Large-format newspaper page the size of The Times or the Daily Telegraph.

"BUSTING". A headline that is too long to fit the space available is said to "bust".

BYLINE. The printed acknowledgement — ranging from a simple line of type to "star billing" complete with photograph — of the authorship of any piece of journalism.

CAPS. Capital letters.

CHARACTERS. Letters, figures, punctuation marks, etc.

CROSSHEADS. Occasional lines of type, usually bigger and bolder than the body-type, which are meant to liven up the page.

DEADLINE. The time by which a journalist must have his story filed if it is not to miss the next edition.

EM, EN. Units of measurement for type, being the width of the letters M or N.

FILE. To transmit copy to the paper.

FONT. A typeface of one particular style and size.

FOURTH ESTATE. Supposedly Fleet Street's place in the established order of things after the Lords Spiritual, the Lords Temporal and the Commons. ("The gallery in which the reporters sit has become a fourth estate of the realm" — Macaulay.)

GOTHIC. An elaborate typeface resembling mediaeval script.

HEAVIES. Popular journalists' faintly derisory term for supposedly serious papers such as The Times and The Guardian.

HOUSE STYLE. Standardised spelling, style of punctuation,

policy on capital letters etc., intended to be followed by everyone on the paper.

INTRO. Opening paragraph.

LEADED. Spaced out to fit the allocated length, literally by inserting blank slugs of lead between the lines of type.

LEG. A length of type as it appears on the page: a story occupying three columns would be said to be in three legs.

LITERAL. A printing error.

LOWER CASE. Small letters, i.e. not capitals.

PAGE SCHEME. A lay-out of a page showing the position of headlines, pictures, advertisements etc.

PAR. Paragraph.

PAY-OFF. The last paragraph of a story, particularly if it contains a final twist or flourish.

POINT (12 point, 144 point etc.). Type measurement on the basis of 72 points to the inch.

QUOTE, QUOTES. Verbatim extract from a speech or interview. Quotation marks.

ROMAN. Plain upright letters (as opposed to italics).

SCREAMER. Exclamation mark.

SPLASH. Main front page story.

STANDFIRST. Introductory matter that is separate from the story or feature itself.

STONE. The table (actually of metal) on which the page is assembled from type and photographic blocks.

STONE-SUB. The sub-editor who sees the type put into page form and cuts articles on the spot if they are too long to fit, as well as making last-minute corrections.

SUB. Sub-editor who edits and checks articles and writes the headlines and crossheads.

SUB-DECK. A subsidiary headline.

TABLOID. A newspaper in the format of the Daily Mirror.

UPPER CASE. Capital letters.

WIDOW. A line of type containing only one single word or syllable.

Standfirst

When the Daily Mirror first gave voice it spoke in the celluloid-collar English then common to all newspapers.

In those penny-a-lining days, policemen were upholders of the law, criminals were denizens of the underworld, goalkeepers were custodians of the citadel — and journalists were gentlemen of the Press. They wrote like counting-house clerks forging their own references.

Long after the times had changed, the language of the newspapers had not. This headline tells us that the period is the Twenties: SHORT-LIVED ROMANCE OF WELL-TO-DO WIDOW AND A COCKTAIL SHAKER. But the accompanying report could have been written in the eighteen-nineties: "In the Divorce Court yesterday, Mr Justice Hill granted a decree nisi to Mrs Ellen O'Connor, residing at Lancaster Gate, W., in consequence of the misconduct of her husband ..."

Not many years later, the Daily Mirror became the first British newspaper to revolt against such strangulated prose. The story of how it did so has been well told in Hugh Cudlipp's *Publish and be Damned* and doesn't need to be re-summarised here. It is enough to say that in the mid-Thirties the Mirror spat the plum from its mouth and began to speak in its own voice (although the voice was not averse to the occasional imitation, as a blurb for the Beezlebub Jones strip shows: "Zeke was plumb kayoed by the bonk on the cabeezer which Davy done give him with his wooden laig..." Several decades after Beezlebub's demise, expressions of the *plumb loco* variety are to be found only in old dictionaries of American slang — and in current newspaper headlines).

The Mirror — to borrow some favourite expressions from its new, robust vocabulary — ceased to be fuddy-duddy and became brash and cheeky. Or so it seemed at the time: from a distance of forty years, its snappy captions now have the wistful charm of old sepia photographs:

WELL, OF ALL THE LUCK
On the hottest day of the year, these two girls set out for a day's work in a film studio at Denham.

* * *

And found that their job was to be photographed in their undies for the film "Ten Days in Paris."

* * *

And if that isn't luck on a blazing day, we'd like to know what luck is.

Sometimes, it has to be said with hindsight, the paper's efforts to be bright and breezy had all the desperation of a fixed smile, and on occasion it could be so trivial as to appear feather-brained. The self-conscious, over-staccato language, striving to be up-to-date and down-to-earth at the same time, oscillated wildly between the slangy and the streamlined, between the homely and the Hollywood. But at its best it was good, plain, refreshing, vigorous English. It was not, as has sometimes been claimed, "the language of the people," for just as the people had never called criminals denizens of the underworld nor goalkeepers custodians of the citadel, neither did they now call psychiatrists mind-doctors nor drop the definite article from the beginning of sentences ("Box with documents buried 64 years ago has been unearthed during repairs at..."). But it was language the people could understand.

What was just as important: it was language that had a profound effect on journalism. When reporters stopped calling policemen upholders of the law and started calling them cops (in the movie-slang of the day) it was not only Fleet Street's musty terminology they were beginning to question.

The Uriah Heep approach typified by the Mirror's coverage of the 1929 election — "A further succession of Socialist gains was the unhappy tale of yesterday's election results..." — had now gone for ever. Authority was no longer kow-towed to. Institutions were challenged. Emperors wearing new clothes were told unkind home truths. Applecarts were upset. Cassandra, the Mirror's great columnist, was billed as "the terror of the twerps." Sledge-hammer text accompanied pile-driver headlines. And when not engaged in its favourite pastime of taunting the "fuddy-duddies," the paper was indulging in its other celebrated preoccupation of having Fun. (The Daily Mirror periodically pursued Fun with the dedication of an alcoholic on a three-day jag.)

Excitable, exuberant, always vigorous, sometimes vitriolic, the prose style that the Mirror evolved in the course of inventing British tabloid journalism was to remain for several decades its virtual copyright. Few could imitate it (not many wanted to) and those who tried were usually misled by its apparent simplicity into "writing down" to the reader.

Today the Mirror is so widely imitated, or anyway emulated, that there is no longer anything exclusive about its brand of English. When not only other newspapers but television news-readers speak fluent Tabloidese ("Good evening. The dollar takes a pounding"), the copyright may be said to have lapsed. The once unique style is in such general use, indeed, that casual observers may sometimes mistake the copy for the original. But is the original ever mistaken for the copy?

The Daily Mirror has better operators than any of its competitors or would-be competitors. It still has original, sometimes brilliant ideas. Its pages remain fresh and lively. Its pictures continue to lead the field. Why, then, has it not always kept ahead of the pack (though the pack has never been ahead of the leader) in its use of words?

Popular journalism — as H. L. Mencken acknowledges in his scholarly *The American Language,* even though his stuffier counterparts on this side of the Atlantic may not — used to be one of the great invigorating influences on the language (there is a plaque in Times Square to the sports cartoonist who coined *hot dog*). Today it is one of the most deadening influences. With some notable exceptions — not all of them the star writers who have carte blanche to use words like "carte blanche" — the popular newspapers give us, in the immortal words of Ernest Bevin, "clitch after clitch after clitch." And this in an age when ordinary street English grows ever more expressive and colourful.

It is tempting to quote fancy theories about what has gone wrong. One is that we no longer live in a black-and-white world tailor-made for crusading tabloids and that as the issues of the day

11

grow ever more complex, the newspapers retreat into trivia, with a resultant trivialisation of their once trenchant style. Another is that competition has raised the tabloid voice to such a monotonously shrill level that it has lost its impact. (Note that raising the voice is not the same as raising the tone.)

While there is probably something in both these notions, there could be a more mundane explanation. Tabloid journalism is no longer doing anything new. The pioneer days are long over. When journalists arrive on a tabloid paper they no longer have to re-think their reporting or subbing style to its very basics, with that resultant jolt to the creative system that has produced some of Fleet Street's finest writers and editorial technicians over the years. They already know tabloid style, or what they have been told is tabloid style, backwards. They learned it on their very first suburban weeklies. There is not a junior reporter in the land who cannot churn out, "Feathers really flew the night a chicken-sexer got the bird," or "Smoky the cat went on the tiles yesterday — and used up most of her nine lives." Recruits to Fleet Street are entitled to ask what need there is of learning new tricks when the old ones are still so much in demand.

What can be done? The Mirror transformed the language of journalism in or around November 1934. It was as different from the language once used by newspapers as that of commercial radio is from the BBC English of the Reith era. But what is done first can be done only once. Revolutions do not go on happening. There can be only one real revolution, and everything that follows (as the People's Daily of Peking would probably agree) is merely revision.

No Harry Guy Bartholomew, and certainly no Rupert Murdoch, is likely to shake up the popular newspaper as thoroughly as it was shaken up over forty years ago. Someone may invent a totally new kind of paper, but invention is something more than transformation. While the popular, Fleet Street-based, nationally-distributed daily lasts, it will be in something pretty well approximate to its present form.

What it can do is to get better. It can take stock of itself. It can spring-clean. It can throw out much of its cliché-ridden, pun-barnacled vocabulary and invest in a good, modern supply of plain English. It can dismantle ancient, cor-blimey headlines which have became as familiar as the neon signs in Piccadilly Circus. It can re-examine the stereotyped news values that encourage stereotyped writing — and the stereotyped writing that encourages stereotyped observation. It can, in sum, stop selling itself short.

The object of this manual is to start hacking away at the dead wood.

NOTE: What follows is based mainly on a not-very-comprehensive monitoring of the Daily Mirror over a period of a few weeks, with the occasional sidelong glance at the opposition. The examples used are those that were nearest to hand when a particular section was written. In every case, a dozen similar examples could easily have been found; in other words, this was random selection and there was no organised scrutiny of the work of either individuals or departments.

Adjectives

Adjectives should not be allowed in newspapers unless they have something to say.

Red-haired tells us that a person has red hair. *Vivacious* — a word belonging to the lost world of Marcel waves and cocktail cherries — tells us nothing except that someone has sat down at a typewriter and tapped out the word "vivacious."

An adjective should not raise questions in the reader's mind, it should answer them. *Angry* informs. *Tall* invites the question, how tall? The well-loved phrase *His expensive tastes ran to fast cars* simply whets the appetite for examples of the expensive tastes, and the makes and engine capacity of the fast cars.

Adjectives used for effect should not be too clapped-out to evoke anything in the reader's mind: *grim* timetable of death, *vital* clues, *brutal* murder, *hush-hush* inquiry, no longer add very much to the nouns they accompany.

Smothering an intro in an HP sauce of adjectives does little to improve its flavour:

> **Manchester City are poised to sign Wolves'** *brilliant* **midfield man Steve Daley and Wrexham's** *impressive* **striker Bobby Shinton in a** *massive* **£1 million** *double* **deal.**

Massive, like *double,* is tautology, and remains so when we learn later that "the Maine Road club" (see INELEGANT VARIATION) are determined to push through the *massive* deal that would involve £850,000 for Daley and £350,000 for Shinton. Then we are told that other clubs have been keen on the *impressive* Shinton. The repetition of an already inessential adjective is lame.

For a profession that is supposed to be hard-boiled, journalism is remarkably chivalrous with its adjectives. Models are *attractive* or *stunning,* or they are given the accolade of *top* (see THE TOPS), or they are *curvy* — which seems to have come into vogue when someone realised that *curvaceous* was getting long in the

14

tooth. (So is *curvy*, by now.) Small young women are *petite*. Small old women are *tiny*. Young men are often *dashing* — an anyone-for-tennis word from the same era as *vivacious*. There are few ordinary housewives, but *model* housewives abound. The Mirror has even given us a *model* soldier:

Model soldier John Jones is being made homeless — by the army.

Long experience of the Mirror's weakness for model house-wives arouses suspicions that this is not a story from Toytown.

Model, of course, is strictly speaking not an adjective but a noun. A glance at any day's paper (**MIRACLE** WIFE WHO 'DIED', **DANGER** FOOD FIRMS RAPPED, **DREAM** TRIP TO PARADISE) will show that nouns are used as adjectives far more than adjectives proper. There is nothing wrong with that: a considerable acreage of pulp forest must have been saved over the years by the use of *flight chaos* as shorthand for *chaos caused by a strike of air traffic controllers* (but see TABLOIDESE and RANK AND FILE). But the cautions expressed at the beginning of this section still apply. Bearing in mind that an adjective by any name still has to earn its keep, a noun used as an adjective should ideally make a statement rather than raise a question.

Dawn swoop, though a choice example of Tabloidese, makes a statement: it tells us roughly at what time of day the swoop was made. *Surprise swoop* raises the question, who was surprised? (It is also tautology, since swoops are not usually made by appointment.) *Shock swoop* is as bad as surprise swoop, with the bonus fault that *shock* is a much-over-used noun-adjective (*shock* report, *shock* move etc.).

Another over-used noun-adjective is *luxury*. Is it worth mentioning that a Saudi Arabian prince lives in a *luxury home?* We would hardly expect him to live in a barrel (which would be worth a line or two). But his *25-bathroom home* or his *£250,000 home* would be informative. (*Luxury* has been for so long used as an adjective that we have forgotten the proper meanings of its legitimately adjectival offshoots. The Mirror invited competition winners to relax *luxuriantly* for a week on palm-fringed sands. *Luxuriant* means abundant or exuberant in growth. A *luxurious* week would have been a better offer.)

Miracle is also over-used. The Mirror has vouchsafed so many miracle wives, miracle mums, miracle babies, miracle cures and miracle escapes that an apposite consolation prize for competition runners-up not qualifying for a luxuriant week on palm-fringed sands could well be a year's supply of loaves and fishes, at no cost to the management.

And

We were taught at school that we may not begin sentences with "And."

Then we were taught in newspaper offices that we may.

And quite right too. But newspapers so overdo it that they sometimes read like the New English Bible:

> As temperatures in the city soared to 81F, it just wasn't a day to quibble about the Budget's 2p extra on a pint.
>
> *And* the hottest favourite at Royal Ascot was a chilled bottle of bubbly — at £19.50 a time.
>
> The top-hat-and-tails brigade sweltered in the sun.
>
> But the Queen clearly didn't reckon it was a day for dressing up.
>
> She stayed cool in the same outfit she wore on her trip to Saudi Arabia in February.
>
> *And* she cut 2ft off the hemline to give it a new look.
>
> The only people not revelling in the sun yesterday were hay-fever sufferers.
>
> The pollen count in the South East soared from a sniffling 33 — to an eye-watering 145.
>
> *And* the heat has also taken its toll on the Continent.
>
> The Greeks are being grilled by temperatures of 100F.
>
> At least thirteen people have died of sunstroke.
>
> *And* it's like a Turkish bath in Istanbul...

Besides being a near-perfect example of the chirpy weather round-up (see THE WEATHER-VANE) this extract very well illustrates a common application of *And* — which is to round the edges of a piece that would otherwise have had too many sharp corners, caused by a succession of monotonously unvarying short sentences. The four *Ands* could be removed from their present positions and placed in front of four other sentences, more or less at random, without affecting the story in any degree.

And is also commonly used to round off a sequence of events where the story takes a narrative form ("*And* last night the 35-year-old company director fell into bed — for a three-day rest"). Or it is used to split an over-long intro into two paragraphs ("*And* last night police were hunting three youths") — which might well be a way of dealing with the objection raised in Hecht and MacArthur's *The Front Page:* "Who the hell ever reads the second paragraph?"

It cannot be said that *And* is often wrongly-used, but it becomes tedious when over-used. If the story eats *Ands* as a worn-out engine eats lubricating oil, try an overhaul.

(See also CONSEQUENCES)

...And that's a cliché

By crossing out — say — *according to a report of the Office of Population Censuses and Surveys* and substituting *and that's official,* it is possible to remove nine dead words from an intro, so that we get:

We're living in luxury — and that's official . . .

(The boring attribution can be slipped in towards the end of the story.)

Thus someone must have reasoned when tabloids were in their infancy. Rightly so: tedium is to be avoided.

But over a period of 45 years, *and that's official* has become in itself typical of the kind of phrase the Mirror ought to avoid. It is terribly hackneyed by now — and it tends to fossilise this type of story so that it remains perpetually in a period when it was the fashion to start with an attention-grabbing generality and justify it later with facts.

Any convention that stops a newspaper's style from evolving should be dropped.

The asthmatic comma

It is not the function of the comma to help a wheezing sentence get its breath back. That, however, is how the comma earns much of its living in daily journalism:

> **Holidaymakers, who turned up in their hundreds to watch the sizzling sequel to their neck-and-neck first round 64s, saw Gallacher jet away with it.**

Neither of those commas should be there — except that the sentence would turn purple in the face without them. Moreover, by demoting the arrival of the holidaymakers to a subordinate clause, they subtly promise a more exciting ending to the sentence than we are about to get.

The semi-colon, too, is often used as breathing apparatus. In the following example, semi-colons have applied the kiss of life — and failed:

> **When a group of children appear who are five times as likely to go to University as the national average; and when it turns out that all their mothers received a certain type of medical treatment before the children were born; doctors sit up and take notice.**

This is wildly wrong. Semi-colons simply cannot be used as souped-up commas in this way. But even correct punctuation could not save this sentence. There is really nothing to do with it except demolish it and start again.

Here is how a healthy sentence can get by without either of these aids, so long as it keeps its nerve:

> **Manchester United manager Dave Sexton postponed the announcement of his FA Cup Final line-up for a second time yesterday in the hope that master striker Jimmy Greenhoff might yet win his five-week fitness battle.**

Here is what happens to an equally healthy passage, of shorter length, when it loses confidence in itself (or when someone handling the material has no confidence in it):

20

> My father was a divorce barrister. When he came home from work he'd sit on the end of my bed and, instead of fairy stories, would give me accounts of his triumphs in the Courts.

On the other hand, it is not unheard-of for an independent-minded sentence to refuse the help of a comma even when one is manifestly needed:

> Torrential rain knocked out yesterday's racing at Epsom and a seven o'clock inspection this morning will decide if today's programme can go ahead.

Here we have two sentences masquerading as one, with the bridging *and* trying to bamboozle us into thinking that no punctuation is necessary. But it is. Until we near the end of this compendium sentence, we are being led to believe that torrential rain knocked out both the racing at Epsom and the seven o'clock inspection.

Moral: a sentence that obliges the reader to revise his opinion of what it is saying should be re-cast.

By and large, however, the Mirror's punctuation sins are those of commission rather than omission. There is a touching belief that bad construction can be cured by sprinkling the offending passage with commas:

> Child-minders, are getting together to increase the number of toy libraries. Community-minded mothers are setting them up and, while children play and pick from the selection of toys unrestricted by the limits of family budgeting, their mothers, too, find companionship.

The comma after *child-minders* must be a literal: but in a piece with more commas than a roly-poly pudding has currants, it was probably overlooked. The comma after *setting them up and* is a gesture of despair: recognising that the construction is so awkward that it makes reading the passage a nasty experience for the reader, the comma does its futile best but then washes its hands of the entire sentence. Given the grotesque shape of the sentence, the remaining commas are appropriate — just as a steel brace would be appropriate for a twisted back. Taking the punctuation of this example as our criterion, let us see how another passage might have appeared in the Mirror:

21

At the end, after one of the most exciting FA Cup semi-finals I have ever seen, they trooped away, still quivering with the exhaustion that springs from unbearable tension, and unforgettable emotion.

Here is how it did appear — in the hands of a stylist:

They trooped away at the end still quivering with the exhaustion that springs from unbearable tension and unforgettable emotion, after one of the most exciting FA Cup semi-finals I have ever seen.

The single comma, which is all this confident construction needs, not only does its basic job of clarification, it contributes towards the dramatic effect of the sentence. Elsewhere, the very *absence* of commas helps the rhythms that give this passage its air of excitement.

There is no space in this manual for a summary of the rules of punctuation, but a few random principles may be stated:

1. Never use punctuation marks to lend respectability to a sentence you would not otherwise care to introduce to your mother.

2. Beware the misplaced comma which distorts meaning, as in: "Though to be fair, the Swedes defended stubbornly." Nice of the Swedes to be fair in this way, the reader might think. If it was the reporter who wished to be fair, he would have needed an extra comma after *though*. Probably he could have borrowed one from a later sentence: "It has to be stressed that this was a friendly match, in every sense of the word, with both sides allowing the midfield men room to work." Which leads us to:

3. Commas are not condiments. Do not pepper sentences with them unnecessarily.

4. Once a series of semi-colons has been embarked upon, there is no going back:

John Conteh, Somerset captain Brian Rose and Malmo manager Bobby Houghton all come under fire this week. Conteh, for his modest performance against the unranked American Ivy Brown; Rose for his infamous declaration in the Benson and Hedges Cup game at Worcester and Houghton for his team's negative tactics in the European Cup final against Nottingham Forest.

There should be a semi-colon after *Worcester*. It has been left out as being superfluous. It isn't — for without it, the remarks about Houghton are a continuation of the remarks about Rose, and this catalogue sentence is grammatically incomplete. But it was that to begin with: it should have been linked with the *come under fire* preamble by a colon, rather than separated from it by a full stop.

5. As in GRAMMAR (qv) many errors of punctuation are the result of carelessness rather than ignorance. The basic rule of thumb, "If it feels right it probably is right" should serve those who have become a little hazy on the difference between a participial phrase and an absolute phrase. When in doubt, ask these questions: What is this comma/colon/semi-colon doing here? What is its job? Is the job being properly done, or is it just a bit of patchwork? Should the job be done by a punctuation mark at all, or is the comma/colon/semi-colon fulfilling the role of a six-inch nail supporting a badly-fitting dovetail joint?

(See also DOTS AND DASHES)

Below the belt

Fleet Street finds it difficult to handle a story about knickers with a smile instead of a snigger.

WENDY'S SIX-KNICKER FINE

Wendy Richardson had a brief reply to a demand for a £6 parking penalty.

She was so incensed that she wrote a "cheque" on a pair of silk French cami-knickers and sent them to the local fines office.

Miss Richardson, a 26-year-old wages clerk of Ward End Road, Birmingham, had been shopping with her mother and returned to her car to find it had been booked...

Thus the Daily Mail. *Six-knicker* in the headline has the merit of being an apposite pun. *Brief* in the intro is more forced. But the story then continues in a straightforward manner. So it should. It is an amusing little item and doesn't need touching up.

The same story as treated in The Sun:

KNICKERS! WENDY'S CHEEKY CHEQUE...

Wendy Richardson really got her knickers in a twist when she was nicked for parking.

She just snapped when she got a £6 fine... and scrawled out her cheque on a pair of French bloomers.

Wendy, 26, says her message to the authorities was very clear: Knickers...

We are on familiar ground. Ladies' underwear, bodily functions and private parts have a chortling fascination for schoolboys — and popular newspapers.

The Mirror goes lavatorial:

A town hall's female staff felt proper peeved when passing housewives kept popping in to use their loo.

And their tempers finally reached flush point when they found one hot and bothered shopper cooling down in their wash basins...

Stories such as that verge on self-parody.

Stories dealing in a tee-hee manner with backsides ("Girls get to the *bottom* of a new craze" etc etc) are too numerous, and too unhumorous, to mention. (But what is worth mentioning is that Fleet Street, with its arch obsession with bums, has done for the adjective *cheeky* what homosexuals have done for *gay*: made it unsafe to use in its original sense.)

Considering how the Third Form of the Fourth Estate reacts to bottoms, lavatories and knickers, it is perhaps as well that there are not many news stories involving district nurses' bicycle seats.

Captions

Caption-writing is a branch of literature that the popular newspapers have made all their own.

Where else could one read:

COLLECTOR'S ITEM

Pretty Pippa Forrest is an old-fashioned girl at heart. She has an old English sheepdog called Emma... and a passion for antiques. Pippa, 22, who comes from East Sussex, specialises in collecting old oak furniture. Which is hardly surprising, when you think of it, with a name like Forrest!

— and the next question is, where else would one want to?

The caption-writer's problem is that he has no more than fifty or sixty words in which to say precisely nothing.

The only real information he starts out with is that his subject is a real pet when it comes to caring for animals, or that the 21-year-old stunner is a home-loving girl at heart, or that early birds at the Sussex seaside can glimpse jaunty Jane most mornings on her newly-bought bicycle. Neither the model's cats (which help to keep her kittenish) nor her flat-decorating activities (which make her surroundings more attractive) nor her bicycle (which prevents her having a spare tyre) actually figure in the picture. The best the caption-writer can do is to embroider a mini-essay around the kind of arch smalltalk heard from MCs of the Miss World contest when told that Miss Venezuela is fond of travel and makes many of her own dresses.

The jaunty caption goes back well into the days when the girls kept their clothes on. Twenty years ago, for some now obscure reason, nautical themes were much favoured, with *Show a leg there!* being a common intro. Although the pictures have changed over the years, the captions have made little progress. It is as if someone has decided that this art-form is as perfect as it ever will be, and that further development is impossible.

Certainly it must be difficult to write fifty attention-grabbing words when the picture is already engaging the reader's interest to the full and the only information he really wants is not of the kind that appears in family newspapers. But that is no reason why the style of the caption should be set in aspic. After all, if back in those *Show a leg there!* days it had been the fashion for captions to appear in rhyming couplets or as imaginary conversations between a ship's parrot and the first mate, someone would have demanded a change by now. There is no preservation order on the caption as an ancient monument, and the puns, double entendres and dated roadhouse expressions *(head - turning looks... admirers... dishy... looking great...)* are not doomed to haunt the Mirror's battlements for ever.

Captions that tie up lightheartedly with some general news event such as the weather, the Budget or the Cup Final (so long as the girl involved is not said to look like a winner who is gunning for Arsenal) are off to a better start than those that heartily simulate interest in the model's hobbies and aspirations. Captions that have something to say, of course, should always win over those that do not, although that cannot be taken as a firm principle: *Halo, halo, what's going on here?* on a picture of Ian Ogilvy in his role as The Saint, would do credit to any portrait of a curvy angel who has really been in heaven since her career took wings.

Clichés

When Sam Goldwyn advised that clichés should be avoided like the plague, he forgot that the plague, by its very nature, is almost impossible to avoid. That is what gave the Black Death such a bad name.

Journalism has been contaminated by clichés since the profession began. It always will be. But not, mercifully, the same ones. Old clichés, like old soldiers, may not die but they do eventually fade away — to be replaced by new clichés.

Manuals of journalism published only a few years ago seem quaintly dated when they come to their lists of newspaper clichés — *burning issue, beggars description, like rats in a trap, limped into port, news leaked out, fair sex, speculation was rife* and so on.

Most such phrases would not be given house-room in a modern newspaper. But when we notice what *is* given house-room, it is evident that the cliché-plague is not only still with us but that it is all the time developing powerful new strains resistant to any known antidote.

Clichés should be avoided by writers in general because reach-me-down phraseology has no place in original prose. They should be avoided by journalists in particular because it is the tendency of clichés to generalise, approximate or distort. The day will never arrive when newspapers are cliché-free, but the following cross-section of words and phrases could vanish at once without any loss to journalism. (Some of the examples in this selective, very incomplete list have been touched on elsewhere in these pages, but it will do no harm to touch on them again.)

Angels (for nurses)	**Dashing**
Alive and well and...	**Dropped a clanger**
And that's official	**Dream holiday**
Billy Bunters	**Fashion stakes**
Clampdown	**Feathers really flew**
Clown prince	**Flushed with shame**
Curvy	**Fair cop**
Cheeky	**Good buys**

Giantkillers
Hammered
Hurtle
Helluva
Hello sailor
Inch war
Knickers in a twist
Love-tug
Love-child
Merry widow
Nationwide hunt/search
Oo-la-la *(this foreign-desk
phrase, believed to be
extinct, was sighted
recently in The Sun)*
Petite
Pay bonanza

Purrfect (for cats)
Pinta
Rampage
Rapped
Sin-bin
Slammed
Slapped a ban
Sweet smell of success
Soccer clash
Spree
Sir (for teachers)
Take a letter, Miss Smith
There's an awful lot of coffee
Tragedy struck when
Trouble flared when
Vivacious
Writing on the wall

Note: In an era of radical change, clichés are now vulnerable not only to old age but to technological and social progress. *Gymslip mums,* for example, must have given way to *jeans and T-shirt mums* by now, and today's *carbon-copy deaths* are surely *photocopies.*

Consequences

Probably few practitioners of modern journalism realise that the ground-rules for the narrative or human interest story peculiar to popular newspapers ("It was gnash, fang, gollop, the day Gilbert the Pyrenean mountain dog tried to escape from a locked car...") were laid down in *Cassell's Book of Indoor Amusements, Card Games and Fireside Fun* in the year 1881.

The time-honoured game from which the rules derive is *Consequences.* Its method of play — a formal sequence of adjectives, names, places, happenings and statements (or quotes), followed by "the consequence" and "what the world said" — is remarkably similar to the way perhaps nine out of ten human interest stories are structured.

The classic opening for Fleet Street's parlour game is a short summary of *what resulted* ("It was one darn thing after another") followed by *when* ("the day" or "the night") followed by *adjectives and name* ("27-stone Bessie Bottomley") followed by *event* ("lost her knitting needles") followed by *where* ("down the plughole in a superstore's ladies' loo").

The narrative then proceeds chronologically, each step being strictly governed by a preposition or conjunction such as *For, And, But, So:*

For (expands on what resulted: Bulging Bessie puts plump finger down drain and gets stuck);

And (continues to expand on what resulted: only way she can get free is by ripping sink off wall);

But (new development promised: Bessie's heart *sinks* — or blood *drains* from face — when she is stopped by store detectives);

For (new development takes place: Bessie goes *round bend* when arrested for shoplifting sink);

So (and the consequence was: Bessie's court appearance, still with sink stuck on finger);

And (and the world said: quotes from magistrate, Bessie and department store spokesman).

Consequences is a harmless game unless (as often happens) it is played three or four times in the same issue, when its deficiencies as a modern indoor amusement or piece of fireside fun become apparent. Its structure — with the obligatory *Ands* and *Buts* and *Fors* corseting the narrative like iron girders — is altogether too rigid for a type of story that ought to bounce and bubble along. Moreover, the predestined, step-by-step approach often drags the story out beyond its natural length.

The chronological narrative may be the best way of telling a human interest story, but that doesn't limit the storyteller to a particular style. The paper certainly has no particular commitment to the set *Consequences* opening, which although it usually succeeds in grabbing the reader's interest then invariably leads him along the well-trodden *For — And — But — So* path.

Consequences should be played much more sparingly — and it should not be played at all when the game cannot be followed through:

> **Villagers felt sore when the gun-slinging dentist went on the rampage.**
>
> **There was a fearsome gnashing of teeth as shots rang out from his garden.**
>
> **And sometimes the dentist, Peter Worledge, shot his mouth off — swearing at the villagers.**
>
> **But yesterday the armed gun-man was rounded up for causing "fear and annoyance."**
>
> **He told a court that he would keep the peace for a year in the village of Hazlingfield, Cambridgeshire.**
>
> **Magistrates at Melbourn heard that Mr. Worledge often fired his shotgun. But the worst time was one Sunday when his neighbour was chopping wood...**

At this point it dawns on us that the narrative we have just read was not a true narrative at all, but simply an elaborate preamble consisting of selected highlights from the gun-slinging dentist's saga, which now commences in earnest and goes on for another four paragraphs, in the course of which it repeats everything we have already been told. The game of Consequences has become the game of Whispers.

(See also NOW READ ON)

Crossheads

Crossheads infest some newspapers more than others.

On a day picked at random — June 22 1979 — the Sun, in a 32-page paper, had 64 crossheads. Only one editorial page — the TV programmes page — was crosshead-free.

On the same day, also in a 32-page paper, the Mirror had but twenty crossheads, and thirteen editorial pages had no conventional crossheads at all.

The crosshead was born in an era when newspapers had titles like The Sporting And Police Gazette or Lloyd's Weekly News. It was introduced to give the reader, and very likely the printer, a periodic relief from eyestrain induced by endless tracts of tiny blurred type devoted to "Extraordinary Charge of Drugging and Violence" and such matters. The crosshead was then a primitive device (it still is). It consisted merely of a few words of copy, usually in body-type and always integral to the text, centred and leaded where they fitted into the story. Since the crossheads could not have been omitted without damaging the text, they could at least be said to have earned their keep.

With improved typography and the development of newspaper make-up, the device became more ornamental than functional. Had the crosshead not existed, tabloid newspapers in particular would have had no need to invent it.

There is something absurd about spattering a page not much bigger than a sheet of foolscap with odd words apparently picked from the dictionary with a pin. *Report, Wine, Corns, Cancelled, Peel, Public, Talk* are from the Sun's bumper crop mentioned above: none of them informs the reader or tempts him to read on. (It is even more absurd when the paragraph to which the crosshead refers has been dropped on the stone, as often happens.)

The Mirror has shown that a well-made-up tabloid can get by virtually without these cryptic aids, especially in features material where there is an abundance of alternatives (which need not be THE INCREDIBLE BLOB, qv) available.

Where crossheads are necessary, however, they are worth more attention than they sometimes get. The standard Mirror crosshead consists of one word, usually of no more than seven or eight characters. The temptation is to assume that any old word will do. It will not.

Abstract nouns that relate to human behaviour *(Sorrow, Theft, Attack)* are better than abstract nouns that don't *(Role, Magic, Nights)* and infinitely better than most concrete nouns *(Table, Coach, Lamp)*.

But verbs or adjectives may be better still. *Stole* is better than *Theft,* night lawyers allowing, and *Hot* is better than *Heat.*

A set of crossheads shouldn't stray from one word-class to another — from a noun to a verb to an adjective, for example. *Sorrow — Stole — Hot* has no logic, and is therefore vaguely disturbing even though the reader can't spot what's amiss.

Sometimes — in big features rather than news stories — the chance comes up for a set of crossheads to be brushed with a little wit. Alliteration *(Hot, Hazy, High)*, word-association *(Faith, Hope, Charity)*, comparatives *(Good, Better, Best)* and suchlike harmless indulgences may not be in the Stone-sub of The Year Award class, but they are an improvement on *Report, Wine, Corns.*

Titillating crossheads — *Whips* (when a scrutiny of the body-type reveals a harmless reference to the House of Commons voting arrangements) — are best left to the successors to The Sporting And Police Gazette and Lloyd's Weekly News. Which is where we came in.

Does all this matter?

Yes.

Every word that appears in the Daily Mirror, from the splash headline to the most obscure clue in the Quizword, has a byline — the byline of the Daily Mirror.

The pitch of the Mirror's voice reveals what it thinks of its readers. The voice-range runs from respect (the Mirror at its best — see WHAT IS STYLE?) to apparent contempt (the Mirror at its worst — see FACETIOUSNESS and other headings).

More important: the Mirror's voice tells readers what they should think of the Mirror. Is it an interesting paper? An important paper? A silly paper? An essential paper? A paper worth buying every day? A paper worth cancelling?

The constantly-revised answers to such questions are to be found in the thirty or forty thousand words of the Mirror's daily output. That is why this manual is considering that wordage in detail.

Dots and dashes

Two news items. Same day, same paper, same page:

Kids today have a driving ambition — and it's NOT with British Rail...

Florists stole wreaths and flowers after funerals... then sold them for a second time to other mourners...

Had the journalist handling the first story handled the second, and vice versa, they could very well have read:

Kids today have a driving ambition... and it's not with British Rail...

Florists stole wreaths and flowers after funerals — then sold them for a second time to other mourners...

Dots and dashes, in Fleet Street if not in the fastidious world outside, are regarded as interchangeable. That suggests there is some vagueness about how they ought to be used.

These are some of the proper uses of dots:

1. Where a sentence tails off because the ending of it is already familiar to the reader, as in *A fool and his money...*

2. Where the writer wants to suggest that there is more that could be said on the subject, as in *But that's another story...*

3. Where a sub-deck, like the verse of a song, leads into the chorus-headline, as in *Thanks to the lads.. WE'RE HOME* (Moment of joy for superstar Elton John).

4. Where (usually in a quotation) some words have been omitted, as in *This brilliant play... should run and run and run.*

5. Where a quotation is not completed, as in most of the examples given here.

These are some of the improper uses of dots:

1. Where the dots should be a dash, as in:

Stand by for the best Easter present of all... some bright weather to shoo away those winter blues...

and:

Brunette Jennifer White went down to the woods... and got horse-whipped...

and:

A teenager girl lies dead on the pavement... the victim of a savage knife attack yesterday on her way to work...

2. Where the dots are in effect saying "Wait for it" before the chortling pay-off is delivered, as in *The lovesick dentist's dowry to his bride was...* (wait for it) *a mouthful of gold teeth.* (Where we have to wait for it, it is worth asking whether it's worth waiting for.)

3. Where the dots are simply added as makeweight to a headline that is too short. (FAREWELL MY LOVELY, if it didn't quite fit, could well read FAREWELL MY LOVELY.. Note that there are two dots, not three. This Mirror house-style — since copied — apparently stems from a senior executive asking, when presented with a headline "busting" by one dot: "But who has laid it down that three dots are mandatory?" Had this lateral thinking embraced the whole three-dots tradition, most of the notes under this heading would not be necessary.)

Some of the proper uses of dashes:

1. As above, where dots have been wrongly used.

2. As parentheses, as in *Later — in a speech at Harold Hill, Essex — Mr. Callaghan said...*

3. In headlines as attribution, as in *Let bombers hang — Police.*

4. As an additional, surprising twist to a sentence, as in *Train fares look certain to rise again this summer — despite British Rail's £58 million profit last year.*

Some improper uses of dashes:

1. The dash standing in for missing words:

The court at Slough, Berks, heard that the Colonel had a string of glamorous lady friends — and installed his favourites in palatial houses.

The mystery of why the court should want to do this expensive favour for the Colonel is cleared up when we realise that the dash, in combination with the *and,* is doing service for *and that he.* This is no part of a dash's job.

2. Dashes standing in for commas. *Sharon Young — who starred in TV's "On The Buses" series — said at her home in Chiswick...* The dashes are here used as parentheses, but the sense calls for commas rather than brackets. *Yesterday Mrs. Whitbread — the 78-year-old Colonel's second wife — said...* Again: parenthesis use of dashes, where commas would have been better. The point here seems to be simply to break up the type. Yet on the next page to this example we have: *There, the refugees, including bewildered young children, were greeted by kindly ladies from the Red Cross.* A couple of dashes could have relieved the great pressure being put on some of the commas in that passage.

Finally, and studiously ignoring the dangerously-high pun-content (see PUNS AND WORDPLAY) in the following story:

> **Shaggy sailor John Holmes was cut to the quick by his shipmates. They called him Veronica because of his long hair. But the unkindest cut of all for John was when an officer picked up the scissors — and went scalp-hunting on the good ship Mohawk.**

The dash, if it has any purpose at all, is a punctuation mark. Punctuation is among other things about pauses. There is absolutely no reason to pause in the above passage, since the effect that could have been made by pausing is spoilt by the words going on for longer than they should. *Picked up the scissors — and went scalp-hunting* would have been right within the lights of this story. *Picked up the scissors — and went scalp-hunting on the good ship Mohawk* goes on a beat too long. Moral: if you don't know where to stop, don't start.

Dramatic events drama

If a news story is dramatic, the drama should come out in the telling. It is not enough simply to assure readers that the drama was there. Such phrases as *dramatic dash, took a dramatic turn* etc. in the text, or *DASH DRAMA* in the headline, are no more than labels to let the reader know what type of story he is reading. They do not convey the drama to him — any more than *funny walk, took a funny turn* or *DASH JOKE* would make him laugh.

By the same token, *colourful* places and characters should be seen to be colourful, not just asserted as such.

Facetiousness

Several of the examples quoted below would be equally at home in PUNS AND WORDPLAY (which should be read in conjunction with this entry). The pun, however, is as essential an ingredient of facetiousness as sugar is of candy-floss, and so some overlapping is inevitable.

What is facetiousness in newspapers, and what is it for? The most accurate definition is probably that it is a form of sustained banter. It joshes the reader from sentence to sentence, rather like an old-fashioned club comedian. (An amusing way of whiling away a dull morning is to go through the worst of the day's crop of facetious stories, interpolating such expressions as " 'Ere, lady!", "It's true!", "Listen, missus!", "He did, honest!" and so on between the paragraphs.)

As to its purpose, this probably stems from the deep-seated fear of a once-insecure profession that its readers would probably rather be playing darts than reading their newspapers. The object is to be entertaining *at all costs*. The story should be effortless to read, which means it must look as if it was effortless to write. Such, anyway, is the theory. In fact the facetious story is as often as not the kind of souffle that could be used as a doorstop.

The following example is mercifully not from the Mirror but from the shoddiest of its imitators, the Daily Star. (It is worth pointing out, though, that an imitator has to have an original to imitate. Most of the hackneyed expressions, weak puns and silly jokes here strung together first saw the light on Mirror copy-paper.) The "story" accompanies two pictures of the Boat Race teams — Cambridge conventionally clad, Oxford stripped to the waist:

A CHEEKY STROKE FOR THE BIG RACE

The husky oarsmen of Oxford, bidding for four Boat Race wins in a row, stole a cheeky march on their rivals yesterday.

They were determined to give Cambridge plenty to beef about before today's race.

So after a hectic gym work-out, they showed what they're made of… by baring their chests and setting their muscles a-rippling.

> The power parade made quite a splash — especially with the Dark
> Blues' young female fans.
> But Cambridge decided to play it cool.
> They posed sedately for pre-race pictures... and then quietly
> planned how to pull the plug on their opponents between Putney and
> Mortlake.
> If they succeed, it will be an upset.
> For Oxford are already 6-4 on favourites to coast home for their
> first four-in-a-row since 1912.

In less than 140 words, the Daily Star has managed to incorporate just about every fault and flaw in popular journalism discussed in these pages.

As a newspaper report, this extreme example is of course 95 per cent padding. In 26 lines of type, half of them double-column, it contains one new fact (the betting odds). It contains two old facts from Whitaker's Almanac (Oxford has won three in a row, last four in a row was 1912). The rest of the story simply consists of words loosely evocative of boat races that happen to have been put together in this particular order, but which could have been put in any other order and still made as much sense — which is to say, not much sense at all.

The story is not so much written as assembled. It is a collage of clichés *(Stole a march, play it cool)*, puns and double entendres *(plenty to beef about, showed what they're made of, quite a splash, pull the plug out)*, and slot-machine adjectives *(husky, hectic)*, all bound together with antiquated Fleet Street verbiage, including the venerable *Dark Blues' young female fans.*

It is clear that some unfortunate journalist was here given the task of making something out of nothing. It can be stated as a principle that the less there is in a story, the higher its facetiousness content.

Penelope Keith, the actress, appears in the new edition of Who's Who where she gives her hobby as gardening. Is this news item, summarised in nineteen words, worth 140 words more? Here — to adapt Parkinson's Law — is how the story expands to fill the space allocated:

> I say, how splendid. The world's worst snob, Margo Leadbetter,
> has finally reached the top of the tree.
> Her nibs Penelope Keith, the actress who played snooty Margo in
> BBC-TV's The Good Life, has received the ultimate accolade for

social graces.

She joins the rest of the nation's upper crust in the latest issue of Who's Who.

The top people's directory lists Penelope's hobby as... GARDENING — a subject even Margo would have approved of.

But last night former convent girl Penelope, 37, was keeping a dignified silence over her inclusion in Who's Who.

A family friend said: "Margo would be jolly pleased. It would be one over Mrs Whatshername at the operatic society.

"But I can't speak for Penelope. She is more modest than Margo..."

And so on. It will be noted that we are more than a quarter into this typographical fortune cookie before its slender message is revealed, and that the only development after that is the conjecture of a "family friend" on the possible reaction of a fictitious character in a TV sitcom.

Let it never be said that the Mirror does anything by halves. If facetiousness is required, then it will be facetiousness of a very high order. The following is a piece of high-precision engineering, with the predictability accurate to a thousandth of an inch, the hackneyed phraseology polished like old brass, and puns worn smooth with age gliding smoothly into place like the moving parts in a well-oiled Victorian donkey engine. As a bonus, this beautiful piece of craftsmanship also includes the news that the footballer Kevin Keegan has made a gramophone record:

HEADING FOR A HIT
Goal ace Kevin pops up in a new field

What a turn-up! Soccer idol Kevin Keegan has made his first pop record. And clearly he's let it go a little to his head. The striker's new goal is to score a chart-buster. Which would be a pretty fancy feat for the maestro of fancy footwork.

But Kevin, who's always on song for his club Hamburg, knows his showbiz career could take an early bath.

"I joke about becoming a singer," he said defensively in London yesterday.

"But if the record does make it, I'll be delighted."

Kevin's disc is called Head Over Heels In Love. And he used top stars Smokie as a backing group.

Which, if you want to get to the top, must be the right way up.

Readers wanting to know what is meant by *always on song* and *if you want to get to the top, must be the right way up* would be missing the point of facetiousness as an art-form. It would be like asking the meaning of a painting by Jackson Pollock. The words do not, taken out of context, mean anything. They do not mean anything when left in context, either: but it should be apparent what they are there for. They are there to keep the wordplay bouncing along, to prevent the text flagging for even a tenth of a second. That is the whole secret of facetiousness.

We have dealt with stories that contain facetiousness and little else, as a balloon contains air. The technique is often used in stories that could very well stand up without it:

CHEERS! WINE IS JUST THE TONIC

Sparkling news, chaps! Uncork a bottle and raise your glasses to the vintage years ahead.

If your favourite tipple is wine, your health prospects are rosy. But for goodness sake lay off the hard stuff.

Experts have discovered that wine — a little of which has always been good for the stomach — can also ease the strain on the heart.

A team from the Medical Research Council studied the drinking habits of eighteen countries.

And they report in the Lancet journal that the more wine a nation drinks, the lower the death rate from heart disease among middle-aged men...

A sensation of *déjà vu* would be understandable at this point. A feature of stories written in this style is that the news has to be presented twice — the funny version followed by the more or less straight version.

Without the same generous allocation of space at our disposal, it is time to bring these examples to an end and summarise the case against facetiousness:

1. Sustained facetiousness is evidence of warped editorial judgment. It is right that stories should be allocated space and prominence according to their potential reader-interest, but that should not be the only yardstick. Where it is the only yardstick, and no judgment is made on the treatment, quality or content of a story, then the paper is bound to find itself devoting valuable column inches to potential and nothing else. In other words, it is printing the shopping list instead of delivering the goods — as in the Who's Who story, which might be worth eight inches with

some good quotes from Penelope Keith, yet still gets eight inches without any quotes from her at all.

2. If proper editorial judgment is not used, then facetiousness will flourish and there will always be a market for it. Professional journalists will always tailor their material to the market. The demand for the product therefore creates the kind of cynical outlook embraced by the familiar disclaimer, "This is what they want, this is what they'll get."

3. Facetious writing is nothing more than padding or verbiage. The only case ever made out for padding in journalism ceased to be valid when newspapers stopped paying their contributors at the rate of a penny a line.

4. Facetiousness is not witty — for all that a well-honed pun may cause mock-groans of appreciation among readers as far away from Fleet Street as Ludgate Circus. It is not intellectually clever. It is a mechanical trick. In extreme cases, it can become the verbal equivalent of a nervous tic. It is also very irritating to onlookers. Like children obsessively droning "Wall, tall, fall, call, small, ball, hall," its perpetrators must finally reduce their audience to fury.

5. Soft-core pornography is supposed to encourage a taste for hard-core pornography. Here the process is reversed. Hard-core facetiousness encourages soft-core facetiousness. It will, unless checked, ultimately sweep through the paper like elm-blight. To a great extent, it is doing so already, for pieces that are not, overall, written in the facetious style may often be found to be tainted with facetiousness. The final example in this section will serve as an illustration of this tendency.

The Mirror ran a short news story about the owner of a celebrated talking dog being plagued by obscene phone calls. In the headline he was inevitably *hounded* and in the intro he was inevitably being *dogged,* but apart from these initial aberrations the report was straightforward enough. It was an interesting little story that did not need any window-dressing. In the last paragraph, however, after we have been told that the Post Office are now intercepting calls, the dog owner is quoted as saying: "They'll all be barking up the wrong tree now."

This statement, in its context, makes no sense at all. It might just as well have read, "I feel like a glass of water," or "A good cigar is a smoke." The only excuse for using it is that the old saw about barking up wrong trees is connected with dogs, and the story is about dogs. That, in the fantasy world of facetiousness, is enough.

(See also PUNS AND WORDPLAY and JOKE OVER)

Grammar

The Mirror gets no worse marks for grammar than any other paper including the so-called "heavies." But it does not get better ones. A few blots from our copybook (errors italicised, explanations parenthesised):

> **As Britain's first Minister for Sport,** *no-one* **did more at all levels to help British sport.** (Unless we are sneaking in a political judgment here, we cannot really claim that the Minister for Sport was nobody.)

> **If you have something to laugh at, complain about,** *or an experience* **to share, the Mirror wants to hear it.** (The catalogue is governed by *something to,* which requires verbs. *An experience* is not a verb. The Mirror is in good company: the Observer, in a TV preview, made the Monty Python team *"discuss one another, one another's legs, dentistry, stomach complaints, hair transplants, and throw food at the camera"* The catalogue is governed by *discuss,* which requires nouns. *Throw* is not a noun.)

> **Only the lunatic few among** *we* **Somerset members did not condemn Brian Rose's one-run declaration at Worcester last week.** (Most of *us* non-Somerset members would agree.)

> **Races are not particularly exciting for most women, unless** *she's* **one of those who like to pose around the track.** (These singular women appear by courtesy of James Hunt.)

> **By simply showing your baby groups of dots on cards every day** *he will quickly learn to identify the total number of dots.* (Either half of this sentence could be italicised as the error. The person of the first part should be the person of the second part also.)

Most journalists, like most other people, have forgotten all they were ever taught about gerunds, dative cases, present subjunctives and so forth. Fortunately, they have usually retained a grasp of syntax which has become almost instinctive (with a few blind spots).

Looking at the examples just quoted, few would be able to say without reference to an elementary English grammar that the reason Britain's first Minister for Sport appears to be Mr. Nobody, and the baby seems to be showing itself groups of dots, is that the participial phrase does not refer to the grammatical subject. But it should be plain to most journalists that there is something wrong with the construction. Where grammatical errors do occur, carelessness or haste rather than blissful ignorance is usually to blame.

In general, if a sentence feels right, it probably is right. If it seems awkward, then it needs investigation. Where the writer's ear tells him he may be on grammatically shaky ground but he cannot remember the particular rule of grammar that would rescue him, it is often possible to find out what, if anything, is wrong by applying simple tests. Some examples:

Should it be *who* or *whom*? Substitute *he* for *who* or *him* for *whom*, if necessary juggling the words around to accommodate the substitution. *I did not know HE was the Editor* is correct, so *I did not know WHOM was the Editor* is incorrect. *Should I get my expenses from HE?* is incorrect, so *From WHOM should I get my expenses?* is correct. (This should dispose of the genteel idea that *whom* is merely *who* with its little finger sticking out.)

Should it be *he and I* or *him and me*? Try leaving one pronoun or the other out of the sentence for a moment. *Will you meet I?* is obviously wrong. *Will you meet HIM?* is obviously right. So *Will you meet HIM AND ME?* would be the correct form.

Should it be *us* or *we*? Omit the noun that belongs to the *us* or *we* pronoun and see what happens. *Only the lunatic few among WE did not condemn Brian Rose's one-run declaration* doesn't sound right, so it should be *Only the lunatic few among US Somerset members did not condemn...* Where the pronoun is not accompanied by its noun, try adding the repeated verb that is implicitly there. *They are no better than US ARE* can't be correct, so *They are no better than WE* is correct.

Should it be *is* or *are*? Straightforward plurals *(ships and shoes and carpenters)* are easy to handle, but what about when they are not straightforward, and may not be plurals? *A ship, a shoe and a carpenter ARE among exhibits in the Lewis Carroll Museum* sounds right, and is right. (Number of things among exhibits: three. Therefore plural.) *A ship, a shoe or a carpenter IS to be among the exhibits* sounds doubtful, but is still right. (Number of things that will get into the museum: one. Therefore singular.) Further explorations in the *is/are* jungle are unwise without a guide. But two basic rules are:

1. In *neither-nor* or *either-or* sentences, the verb matches the nearest subject. *(Neither the ship, nor the shoe, nor the carpenter, IS among the exhibits.* But: *Neither the ship, nor any of the other things mentioned, ARE among the exhibits.)*

2. But without the *nor/or, neither/either* takes the singular verb, as do *everyone, someone, everybody, nobody, each* etc. *(Although the ship is among the exhibits, neither of the other two things IS.)*

Should it be *compare with* or *compare to?* It depends what the *compare* sentence is doing. If the idea is to put one thing in the same class as another, then *compare to* would be right: *He COMPARED me TO Shakespeare* (i.e., to my advantage). But if the idea is to show that one thing is *not* in the same class as another, in other words to set up a comparison, then *compare with: He COMPARED me WITH Shakespeare* (i.e., to my detriment).

But all these are rules of thumb, and thumbs have a reputation for sticking out when sore. If being "correct" makes the sentence stiff at the joints, it may be better to be colloquial. Nor is there any point in ploddingly doctoring an "incorrect" sentence in order to give it a clean bill of grammatical health. Either a sentence jars or it doesn't; if it does jar, the most sensible course is to reconstruct it altogether.

Some other possible grammatical pitfalls are discussed under WHICH IS THAT?, THE NUMBERS GAME and THE ASTHMATIC COMMA. Meanwhile:

Different from, not different to.

There is no such word as *miniscule.*

It is not all right to make *alright* one word.

Great minds

Great minds do not think alike. Great minds think differently.

The nearest examples to hand of Fleet Street telepathy:

1. A shopkeeper was blacked by four thousand shipyard workers because she put a penny on the price of a cheese roll. The Daily Star reported: "Her 18 pence rolls *cheesed off* a union boss." The Sun reported: *"Cheesed off...* that's shopkeeper Christina Todd." The Mirror reported: "Now granny Christina's business has stumped to nothing — leaving her really *cheesed off."*

2. Predictable Budget headlines:

Daily Mail: HOWE'S THAT?

The Sun: HOWE'S THAT?

Daily Mirror: THATCHER KEEPS HER PROMISE.. AND HOWE!

Daily Express: TAKING OFF — AND HOWE!

(It will be noticed that two of these headlines contain no new information at all, assuming it is general knowledge that Sir Geoffrey Howe is Chancellor.)

3. Daily Mail headline on the court appearance, in handcuffs (not chains) of Major Bob Astles, Amin's British aide: CHAINED.

Daily Mirror headline: CHAINED.

4. The telepathic influence was strong on the day a man was taken to court for signing his electoral registration form "Mr Kermit."

The Express said that council officials were *hopping mad.*

The Sun said: "Mr Kermit gets *hopping mad."*

The Star said: "Kermit went a-courting yesterday... and ended up *hopping mad."*

But the Mirror story began: "Kermit the Frog hopped along to court yesterday", and then told how "Doncaster council frog-marched him before local magistrates."

It was funny and refreshing and, unlike the great thinking behind the Express, the Sun and the Star stories, it didn't run on train-lines.

Heavens to Betsy

With a little patience, a mynah bird might be taught to recite this list of intros to some recent news stories and features:

What a smasher!
I say, I say! A funny thing happened...
Oh, brother!
Cheers!
What a turn-up!
Brr!
Phew!
Cor! Strike a light!
I say, how splendid!
Sparkling news, chaps!
Calling all kids!
Calling all disco fans!
Calling all stamp collectors!

Mynah bird language is carrying simplicity too far.
(See also SCREAMERS! and WHAT HO & ALL THAT ROT)

How say you?

Tick the correct tense:

> **"I have never seen anything like it. They were like animals,"** *said*
> **Mrs. Smith.**
> **"It is the same every Saturday night. They are like animals,"** *says*
> **Mrs. Jones.**

Both should be ticked. Both would be correct (but not in the same story).

Said is used when the witness or spokesman is describing a one-off incident — a fire, an accident, or perhaps (as in Mrs. Smith's experience above) one of those disturbances known to Fleet Street as a *rampage.*

Says is used when the witness or spokesman is describing a constant or generality — something that is always pretty much the same, such as the Bank Holiday takings at the zoo or the traffic jams on the Chiswick flyover or the aforesaid Mrs. Jones's neighbourhood every Saturday night.

Said, covering immediate events, is more often than not appropriate for news stories. *Says,* covering the background, is more likely to appear in a feature or back-up story.

Says may also appear in a feature interview. But when it does, the whole piece should be in the present tense, not only the quotes.

Whether in the present, past or future tense, avoid the inversion as in "Claims Mrs. Jones: 'They urinate in the floral clock.' " This style was popular many years ago when the Daily Express was imitating Time magazine, which then contained so many inversions that the New Yorker finally commented: "Backward ran sentences until reeled the mind." But it is old hat now.

Imaginary rules

Apart from the usual list of spelling preferences and so on, the Mirror has very few rules governing house style. Many of those that are daily observed turn out to be self-imposed, viz:

1. An intro must consist of a specific number of lines according to its position in the paper. (This particularly applies to regular columns, where the paragraphing is made to follow the page scheme instead of the page scheme following the paragraphing.)

2. A new leg cannot commence with a new paragraph.

3. Certain words, such as *university* and *government,* must be given a capital letter irrespective of whether their use is specific or general. (During the EEC elections, the Mirror put a contributor to the absurdity of saying that the European Parliament was not a European *Government* — thus giving the accolade of a capital letter to an institution which does not exist.)

4. Infinitives cannot be split. (They can, where fusing them makes for clumsiness. Some infinitives, as any good writer knows, are all the better for being split. See MEDDLING.)

Each department of the paper has its own non-existent rulebook of non-existent rules. As guidelines, they may serve a purpose. Followed slavishly, they serve only the pedant.

Whether self-imposed or not, rules were made to be broken.

NB: The above dispensation does not apply to anything laid down in this manual. This is the rule that proves the exception.

The incredible blob

Fowler's *Modern English Usage,* Second Edition, revised by Sir Ernest Gowers (1965) expresses no views on the usage of blobs. It is therefore up to this manual to lay down first principles.

Blobs in the Mirror have what city planners would call a multi-purpose use. There are sometimes so many of them that the paper resembles Cook's International Railway Timetable.

A glance at a Junior Mirror page, for example, reveals five blobs:

- One at the start of a boxed announcement;
- One pinpointing a puzzle answer;
- One on a footnote to readers' letters;
- Two in a caption to a football picture where "two top talents" are identified.

There are opportunities for at least fifteen more blobs on the page but it has been sub-editorially decided that enough is enough. The decision ought to have been made at least three blobs earlier.

Blobs should not be inserted into a page of type like plums into a pudding. It is not their function simply to jolly up the text. Nor should they be called upon to celebrate the extraordinary coincidence that two or three successive sentences happen to begin with the same word, such as HE. Blobs have specific uses, the main ones being:

1. To itemise a genuine list or catalogue. (For bogus lists and catalogues, see LISTS.)

2. To mark a footnote.

3. To mark an addendum to a story, as in, say, a comment from the City Editor on a Parliamentary finance report.

4. To itemise a series of examples or anecdotes — the purpose here being to make it clear to the reader when the text is returning to its general drift.

In short, the blob is an aid to clarity, not a cosmetic aid. If it is doing no more for the page than could be done by a squashed fly, leave it out.

Inelegant variation

Most books about the use of words warn writers against *elegant variation* — e.g., "the penultimate month of the year" as another way of saying November.

In the uncouth world of Fleet Street, where space is tighter than in the three-volume Victorian novels from which the textbooks seem to draw most of their examples of living English, elegant variation is not much of a problem. But *inelegant variation* is.

> **Sugar rots your teeth and probably shortens your life. Britain annually devours 2½m tons of the stuff.**

Thus a Daily Express writer who could just conceivably be using *the stuff* in its pejorative sense, as in *stuff and nonsense,* but who if numerous other examples of *the stuff* are any guide, is far more likely to be stuck for a synonym. But why should he want one? By putting a full stop after *tons* he could have saved himself trouble. By recasting those two sentences altogether, he could have taken on more trouble but avoided the problem.

The stuff is not the most clodhopping of journalism's inelegant variations but it is one of the most common. It is our contribution to the commodities market. There is no raw material, from cocoa to zinc, that has not been described as *the stuff* in print. A broker who kept a tally of the number of times *the stuff* has been used for porridge or treacle or tobacco, could set up a flourishing futures market in this flaccid general synonym.

But we can do worse than that:

> **Cheers! Britain is on a beer bender. Last year we drank a staggering 2,000m gallons of mild, bitter and keg — a foaming 40 pints for every pub-crawler.**
>
> **That's nearly seeing double on the hangover figures of five years ago. And elbow-lifting is still on the increase...**

The story is made up, but the style is not. It is possible to go on in that strain for another nine or ten inches without repeating the key words *beer, Britain* and (particularly) *drink.*

Fleet Street has more synonyms for drinking and eating than Roget ever dreamed of. In newspaper stories we are permitted to eat and drink only in the first paragraph. Thereafter we guzzle. We knock back. We put away. We lower. We lap up. We nosh. We chomp. We slurp. We chew our way through. We sink our teeth into. We get on the outside of. We down. We swig.

As often as not, *the stuff* features in these contortions.

Inelegant variation is not by any means confined to food and drink, but these examples will suffice. The mannerism is easily cured. Before conjuring another of these contrived synonyms out of the air, ask what is wrong with repeating the original word. If it sounds stilted, try a pronoun (*it* is surprisingly under-used for so short a word). If it still doesn't seem right, try rephrasing so that the second or third repetition isn't necessary. If this means cutting out a sentence or two, it is probably all to the good: much inelegant variation comes about from spinning a story out beyond its worth.

Italic and bold

Fowler is as reticent on bold type as he is on blobs. But he is positively garrulous on *italics,* the third of this trio of cosmetic failsafes.

"Printing a passage in italics," begins Fowler acidly, "is a primitive way of soliciting attention." Had his newsagent delivered the Mirror instead of the Times Lit Supp?

The Mirror solicits so much attention with its italics that when it comes to their legitimate use — to stress a word, for example — it has to resort to bold type. But since it uses bold type also as "a primitive way of soliciting attention," bold lower-case type is often not enough. It has to be bold caps.

This is typographical inflation.

Let us look at the extravagant use of italics and bold in the Mirror. It does not run to a pattern. On some pages — usually feature pages — every third paragraph or so is set in italics or bold. On others, even though there may be much longer stretches of text, italics and bold are not used at all. But that is the exception, not the rule.

In one 28-paragraph weekly column, five paragraphs were in black and two in italics (and there were three crossheads for good measure. See CROSSHEADS). The seven paragraphs picked out in this way did not differ in any respect from the twenty-one that were set in ordinary Roman. They did not need to be stressed or featured in any special way. A computer programmed to set any one paragraph out of every four in different type from the body-type might have random-selected those seven paragraphs. Or seven others — it would have made no difference.

The rule seems to be: where a story has been going on for four inches or more, set the next bit in a different typeface in case the the sheer monotony of ploughing through 120 words at a stretch should make the reader's mind wander. (Logically, of course, there is no reason why these variants should stop at italics and bold: in a less conservative newspaper, the odd paragraph would be set in Gothic or Billboard.)

The proper uses of italics are too well-known to need summarising. In any case, they are to be found in Fowler, who concludes his italics article on this sour note: "To italicise whole sentences or large parts of them as a guarantee that some portion of what one has written is really worth attending to is a miserable confession that the rest is negligible."

Bold type, however, should be used for just the purpose that Fowler castigates: to draw the reader's attention to the really important or dramatic passages in a longish story.

Italics and bold can be used to good effect as an integral part of a story's presentation. An excellent example is to be found under WHAT IS STYLE?

Individual words should not be set in bold for the sake of stressing them. This job should be given back to italics.

Italics should *never* be let loose on a joke. If the joke is funny, italics will kill it. If it is not funny, italics will simply embarrass it.

Jargon

In The Guardian (but not in the Mirror) we may read: "Derbyshire is into high-speed transport."

In The Observer (but not in the Mirror) we may read: "Journalism input comes almost entirely from agency reports."

This is the kind of journalism input that is appearing daily in American papers: "PanAm reported no upturn in traffic flow yesterday. 'There's been no onrush,' A PanAm spokeswoman said."

Business corporations, in particular, want everyone to speak their unspeakable "in-house" Dalek language. It is steadily insinuating itself into newspapers, but not, it is to be hoped, into the Mirror.

PS But are the Daleks as appalled by our jargon — *bid, probe, mercy dash* etc — as we are by theirs?

Joke over

FACETIOUSNESS (qv) has been dealt with at length. There is one more aspect of this wearisome style, however, that is worth its own heading.

The flippant, facile approach is doubly reprehensible when it is inappropriate to the subject. It is easy, by allowing the narrative to run on the familiar, stereotyped, jocular lines, to appear indifferent or even callous towards the actual human being involved in the "human story."

> **EYES UP FOR A DISASTER!**
> **Bingo fans knew that trouble was on the cards when Margaret Fieldhouse suddenly dropped in.**
> **For Margaret, 46, made her unexpected entrance *through the ceiling*.**
> **A full house of 300 bingo players stared up in astonishment as her legs came crashing through the plaster...**

The temptation to lay on the Bingo terms thick has been resisted. Paragraph three could very easily have read *It was a case of eyes up for a full house when Bingo! LEGS ELEVEN! Margaret's legs came crashing through the top of the shop...*

Despite this admirable restraint, the story for half its length is told in the standard facetious manner. Given the editorial demand for this kind of thing, the flip approach seems justified. After all, falling through a ceiling can — conceivably — be funny. It is the stuff of slapstick.

But in banana-skin comedy, nobody really gets hurt. When somebody does really get hurt, it ceases to be comedy. It is therefore necessary, in the second half of this story, to straighten the editorial face before continuing:

> **Last night, after treatment for a broken leg and injured spine, she was back home in Logwood Close, Wigan, Lancs.**
> **Margaret, who works as a cashier in a cinema above the bingo hall in Wigan, was too upset to talk.**

Perhaps the lady had a good laugh when she read about her mishap in the Daily Mirror.

The next example — showing how facetiousness can trivialise an event which, although minor, is of great importance to the people involved — makes the Mirror appear philistine and insensitive.

First, excerpts from the Guardian's 12-column-inch report:

> **An enraged artist succeded in closing Battersea Bridge, London, for most of yesterday, after he had discovered demolition men tearing down one of his most cherished works.**
>
> **When Mr. Brian Barnes, 34, saw the devastation of his 250ft-long mural on the side of a disused factory, he climbed on to the remains and offered clenched fist salutes to policemen...**
>
> **His wife... claimed the demolition work had been started at about 3 a.m. and virtually completed before protestors realised what was happening.**
>
> **"The mural took about 60 local people two years to complete and it had only been up about six months," said Mrs. Barnes. "It showed a huge broom sweeping away everything people don't like about Battersea, such as polluting factories, office blocks and high-rise flats.**
>
> **"Where the broom had swept clear there were low-rise houses, decent bus services, allotments, riverside walks and play streets..."**

The issues raised in this last paragraph could form the basis of an editorial policy for a vigorous campaigning newspaper. The four-column-inch report in the vigorous campaigning Mirror was headlined A WILD PAINTER DELAYS QUEEN (she was on her way to the Derby). It told how "Battersea Bridge was closed by the rock-throwing antics of temperamental artist Brian Barnes" and related that "Painter Barnes went up the pole after bulldozers smashed a 238-ft wall mural it had taken him two years to complete." To drive home the gag about Painter Barnes going up the pole, there is an underlined crosshead: *Pole.*

Just-so stories

The conclusions reached later in these pages about *really* (see under OH, REALLY?) apply equally to *just,* as in:

Just why is "Alien" giving America the creeps?

Why *just why*? Why not just *why*?

The same questions may be asked about *just who, just how, just what, just when, just where, just one of those things, just good friends, just the job* and *just purrfect,* all of which regularly occupy much-needed space in newspaper columns.

Lists

Dr. Johnson used to walk along Fleet Street touching lamp posts. This mild case of obsessional mania seems to have been transmitted from generation to generation, for Fleet Street's present-day wordsmiths are victims of a very similar neurosis.

They have a compulsion towards *lists*. They cannot stop themselves arranging pieces of copy to resemble mail-order catalogues or railway timetables. They do it on the slightest excuse, leaping on any combination of words that, with the introduction of black capitals, blobs (see THE INCREDIBLE BLOB) or other typographical gimmickry, can be passed off as tabulation:

> A student with sex problems turned his dormitory room into a makeshift operating theatre.
> He PLACED mirrors around the room to get a good view of his work;
> DRAPED sterilised sheets over the furniture;
> WORE a surgeon's mask and gloves and
> SWALLOWED barbiturates as an anaesthetic.

> This means the teachers will
> REFUSE to supervise children at lunch breaks
> REFUSE to take part in outside activities
> REFUSE to use their own cars on school business

> Later Mr. Orlon, a foreman at the building site, told colleagues about the night visit.
> *Then the blacking really started.*
> THE foreman's association decided not to work with Mr. Clapp.
> MOST of the 350 men on the site are being laid off.
> AND Mr. Clapp has taken a week's holiday.

> The entries against the girls' names included disclosures such as:
> ● "Mother ran off."
> ● "Adoption in the family."
> ● "Being treated for psychological problems."

In the first of these extracts, four parts of the same sentence have been arranged in a list apparently because they all begin with verbs; in the second, a list has been manufactured by the unnecessary repetition of REFUSE; in the third, it is not possible to guess from the material supplied why the words THE, MOST and AND have been picked out in bold capitals; and in the fourth, the principle has been followed that where three examples appear in a news story, each example must be preceded by a blob.

Except for the THE—MOST—AND combination, which defies analysis, the extracts quoted above can at least claim some vague affinity with the catalogue principle. There are examples without number of pronouns such as HE, IT, THEY being picked out in black or awarded a blob for no other reason than that they occur twice in successive sentences. Nor is it uncommon to find a sequence of paragraphs given the bold-and-blob treatment when not by any stretch of the imagination could it be called a list or catalogue. (Specialist articles are especially vulnerable to this treatment, it being a tenet of popular newspaper faith that anything written by specialists needs jollying up.)

A side-product of the *list* obsession is the *in-and-out* syndrome:

> **Gardening was too much of a slog for pensioner Daniel Keen. So was looking after a big cage of pet birds.**
>
> **The retired coalman decided to turn over a new leaf — by converting his garden into a plastic paradise.**
>
> **OUT went his 150 geraniums.**
> **OUT went his fifty budgerigars.**
> **IN came plastic flowers.**
> **IN came plastic budgies.**
> **IN came plastic toys and ornaments...**

An index of Mirror stories where IN has come this and OUT has gone the other would make an impressive list in itself.

Typographical signposts indicating a list or catalogue should be used only when the list or catalogue is a genuine one — e.g., the recommendations of a report, the main points of a speech, the contents of a human ostrich's stomach as revealed by an X-ray.

Whether preceded by a blob, asterisk, star, number or any other symbol, the items in a list are still governed by its overall grammatical structure. It should be possible to attach each item in turn to the introductory matter and make a proper sentence.

Sentences should not be sub-editorially inverted, re-arranged or given labels (*BOOST No. 1* etc) to force them into a list sequence.

It is legitimate, and always tempting, to put a chapter of accidents in list form, but it can create difficulties, as in this example (where all the stops except the last one, incidentally, should be commas):

> **During his eight week jaunt Malcolm was:**
> **INVOLVED in a 100 mph road smash.**
> **HELD by a weird religious sect.**
> **ROBBED of his cash.**
> **BEATEN UP by villains and...**
> **JAILED for carrying a penknife.**

The difficulty here is that so much compression has been necessary to get the events into list form that the entire story has to be gone over again:

> **In British Columbia a car in which he was travelling hit a ditch at 100 mph.**
> **In San Francisco he was held a virtual prisoner by a religious sect...**

And so on. The INVOLVED—HELD—ROBBED list, in effect, robs the Mirror's news pages of nine lines.

Little by little

So many little folk are to be found in the Mirror that it sometimes seems to be aimed at leprechauns.

It is true that there are fewer *little old ladies* inhabiting the news columns than there used to be, but there is still a wide choice of little people. The thinking seems to be that in any story about a child, the reader will prefer a vague size category first and the age later:

> **Little love child Zita Icke won £21,000 damages in the High Court yesterday...** (Age of little love child: five — given in fifth paragraph.)

> **When it comes to fighting big, big battles, Little Thumbelina is head and shoulders above the rest . . .** (Age of Little Thumbelina: 15 weeks—given in second paragraph. Real name given in fourth par.)

> **Little Master Miracle goes home from hospital today...** (Age of Little Master Miracle: 3 months — given in second paragraph. Real name given in third par.)

> **Little Emma Williams may not be old enough to drink, but she can go one better than the regulars in her dad's pub...** (Age of Little Emma: newly-born — we learn when she called Time in the third par.)

Children to whom the size-code for some reason doesn't apply (perhaps they are big for their age?) are often described as *toddlers:*

> **Toddler Kevin Carter pulled on his favourite red wellies, went out to play in the garden... and vanished.**

How old is this toddler? See third paragraph. He is two.

In "hard news" rather than "human interest" stories, these cuddly-toy euphemisms are never used at all:

> **A boy aged nine was found brutally murdered last night...**

Four Rhodesians, including a six-year-old girl, have been tortured and shot to death by Rhodesian guerillas in Zambia...

In any story about children, the reader wants to know at once: *How old?* Is it only in hard news stories that this natural appetite for hard facts can be satisfied in the first five words?

Meddling

This is what the columnist wrote:

I have been spending the last few days in the United States. Saw a couple of shows and solved President Carter's energy problem.

This is what appeared in print:

I have been spending the last few days in the United States, saw a couple of shows and solved President Carter's energy problem.

The "correction" — apparently made in the belief that the second sentence lacks a subject (it doesn't: the subject *I* is implied) — robs the passage not only of its style but of its grammar. The fused "sentence", in the form presented, is governed by the auxiliary verb *have,* and one cannot say *I have saw a couple of shows.*

The same columnist, who wishes to remain anonymous, has also been occasionally plagued by the position of the word *only* being changed in his copy. This arises from a common pedantic fear that *only* in the sense of *no more than (I have ONLY one pen)* may be mistaken for *only* meaning *alone (I ONLY have one pen),* or that *only* meaning *as recently as (I bought it ONLY today)* might similarly be confused *(I ONLY bought it today).* In fact the serious possibility of confusion in the reader's mind does not arise very often, and in any case, *no more than* and *alone* can mean substantially the same thing. *Drink to me ONLY with thine eyes* does not differ materially from *Drink ONLY to me with thine eyes.* It just scans better.

The needless repair of split infinitives when they were split on purpose, and are better so, is infuriating enough to the journalist with an ear for English; it is even more maddening when the infinitive was not split (i.e., the separation of *to* from its verb by an adverb, as in *to really meddle)* in the first place. Anyone who thinks that *to be really meddled with* or *to have just meddled* is an example of a split infinitive, should not meddle.

More haste

The standard Fleet Street excuse for shoddy or silly writing has always been that the offending story was written against the clock.

It usually isn't so.

Deadline fever encourages taut, crisp writing with a maximum of facts and a minimum of frills. The straightforward hard news story, phoned virtually straight on to page one, rarely displays any of the faults discussed in this book.

The truly awfully-written story, of the kind that ought to be hung on the walls of schools of journalism as an example of how not to do it, demands time.

The puns have to be sweated over, the laborious intro has to be reworked again and again until it cannot possibly be any more forced, the jocular references have to be carefully strung together like blunt razor blades dangling from a magnet.

For a story about, say, an old lady who was flushed with embarrassment as a result of being locked in a town hall lavatory, and the consequent chain reaction when the council tried to get to the bottom of it, at least four hours should be allowed.

For a late-night train crash killing 100 people, allow twenty minutes.

Neon signs

Blurbs are a newspaper's neon signs. It is surprising how often the wrong words are picked out in lights.

From a Pop Club competition puff:

- **ATTEND the West End Premiere** etc. etc.
- **SEE Patti Boulaye** etc. etc.
- **RETURN home with a Sanyo music machine** etc. etc.

ATTEND, SEE and RETURN are three very dull words to be accentuated. The reader's heart does not quicken when he is invited to ATTEND, SEE and RETURN. The typographical (and editorial) accent should be on the attractions provided.

Not only but also

Not only are the following two paragraphs not paragraphs, but one of them isn't even a sentence:

Not only was this post box fixed with its slot nine feet above ground. For three weeks people put letters in it.

This follows the rule that says: if a sentence is long and dull, chop it in half and throw away the intervening conjunction. If the passage is still too long, make it into two paragraphs.

There is a codicil to the rule, which goes, "And put in a crosshead." The best recent example of how the split-sentence/paragraph/crosshead technique can be used to baffle the reader is from the Evening News:

Not only is some of the compensation offered inadequate.

CHARGED

Before you can find out whether you have been wrongly charged, you have to make sense of your bills.

Now read on

Like *For, And, But, So,* and so on (see AND and CON-SEQUENCES), *Now* is one of the Mirror's favourite little words.

Beware of *Now* when it is really saying *Now read on:*

> The sweet smell of success has turned into a right stinker of a problem for Kathy and Paul Johnson.
> The couple do a roaring trade in the smelliest stink bombs in town at their joke shop in New Street, Worcester.
> But the husband and wife team have upset other shopkeepers — because some of their customers have been letting the bombs off in other stores around the town.
> *Now* some irate shopkeepers have been carrying out revenge raids on the joke shop. The jokers will pose as ordinary customers, buy their stink bombs... and burst the bombs on the shop floor...

In the first three paragraphs, we learn little more than that a joke shop sells stink bombs. *Now* brings us to the point of the story — in paragraph four.

The delayed-drop *Now* is very common, and is often a case of the rules of CONSEQUENCES being bent to accommodate a story that wants to pass itself off as a narrative story but isn't one really.

The numbers game

> The multi-million dollar saga… will be shunted off into the sidings later this month after its ill-starred inaugural run of less than 20 episodes.

Wrong. *Fewer* than 20 episodes.

> Good on Lord Wallace for telling Lord Spene that his plans to keep working mums at home is the wrong approach to unemployment.

Wrong. His plans *are* the wrong approach.

> Here's two Cup Final fans who certainly don't mind revealing their favourite sides.

Wrong. Here *are* two Cup Final fans.

> He was one of those rare people who enjoyed his money, his talent as a musical conductor — and his fame.

Completely wrong — but if it were made numerically correct the sentence would be absurd: *He was one of those rare people who enjoyed their money, their talents as musical conductors, and their fame.*

Plurals and singulars cause much confusion — not least, when one is mistaken for the other. The following notes may be useful (see also *is/are* under GRAMMAR).

Fewer can be counted, *less* cannot (*fewer* sugar lumps, *less* sugar). *Few* can be plural or singular: *there HAVE BEEN FEW/there HAS BEEN A FEW.*

Collective nouns can be singular or plural. Go by the sense. *The Press IS free* is correct, because we are talking about one body. But *the Press ARE debating their freedom,* since one body cannot debate.

Similarly with plural nouns with a singular meaning. *Politics IS the art of the singular,* because one art is one thing. But *Their politics ARE plural* or *His politics ARE not my politics* because here politics are shared or divided.

When the subject is plural but the object is a quantity, use a singular verb: *Fifty-five mistakes IS A LOT of mistakes.* Otherwise:

The verb follows the number of the subject, as in *HIS PLANS ARE the wrong approach.*

None can be either singular or plural, as can *number.* Fowler recommends treating *number* as singular when it has a definite article *(The NUMBER present WAS large)* and plural when it has an indefinite article *(A large NUMBER WERE present).*

To each his own singular: *each, everybody, everyone,* are singular pronouns requiring singular verbs. But *everyone to his or her desk, please* is schoolma'am English. Duck out of this situation if possible, otherwise use singulars as plurals so long as they don't jar.

Where the numbering is correct, but it still sounds vaguely incorrect, as in *Most people's problem is trying to hang on to their money,* recast it.

Oh, really?

The purpose of *really* in amateur doggerel of the "Father sat upon a pin/It really was a shame" variety is to pad out a line that otherwise would not scan.

It is difficult to detect its purpose in professional journalism. Yet a purpose it must have, for why else would it regularly crop up in newspaper stories?

> **Tippling Tug Wilson could *really* take a lot on board. When he pushed the boat out in the boozer, he drank 15 pints a night...**

> **Do-it-yourself fanatic Michael Taylor *really* did for himself yesterday...**

> **Karen, 20, from Middlesex, had spells as a clerk, typist and window-dresser before she plumped for modelling... and now her career is *really* taking off.**

> **Pint-sized John May *really* stirred it up yesterday... by stealing a milk float...**

In each case, *really* could be replaced by such aimless expressions as *actually, quite, definitely, absolutely, well and truly,* or, for the Irish editions, *entirely:*

> **Tippling Tug Wilson could take quite a lot on board...**

> **Do-it-yourself fanatic Michael Taylor well and truly did for himself...**

> **Now Karen's career is definitely taking off...**

> **Didn't pint-sized John May stir it up entirely now...**

Nothing is gained, nothing is lost, by the substitution. Then is *really* really necessary at all?

> **Tippling Tug Wilson could take a lot on board...**

> **Do-it-yourself fanatic Michael Taylor did for himself yesterday...**

Now Karen's career is taking off…

Pint-sized John May stirred it up yesterday…

None of these excerpts now looks quite right. There is a certain flatness there. It becomes apparent that the purpose of *really* is to provide an artificial boost for material — or anyway, the presentation of material — that would otherwise probably not grab the reader.

If news stories were subject to inspection by the public analyst, he would describe *really* as 0.1% additional colouring matter.

One more time

Whoever first put the headline THUGS BUNNY (a twist on the name of a Warner Brothers cartoon character, born 1936) on a picture of a tough-looking rabbit, was an innovator.

Whoever did it next was a plagiarist.

Those who did it for the third, fourth, tenth, twentieth and hundredth times were stereotypists.

The same applies to such evergreens as CLOWN PRINCE, CATCH OF THE DAY and THE GREAT DRAIN ROBBERY — not to mention the seemingly endless variations on DIDN'T HE DO WELL whenever Bruce Forsyth is in the news (culminating, in the Mirror, in DIDN'T HE BOO WELL! Examination of the text reveals, in this case, that he didn't boo at all, and neither, even, did his audience. They hissed. But WASN'T HE HISSED WELL? would have been a little too far removed from the well-worn catchphrase).

Yet even where a headline has become a stereotype, there is always room for one more ingenious twist. Thus, long after THUGS BUNNY, LUGS BUNNY, MUGS BUNNY etc. had ceased to be clever, the Mirror looked at a picture of a rabbit fostering a kitten and headlined it BUGS MUMMY. That was original and funny.

Note: this dispensation does not apply to any variation of PHEW! WHAT A SCORCHER (see THE WEATHERVANE).

Our readers in Wigan

The question, "Will our readers living in Wigan understand this?" is not always a legitimate one.

Where the question is genuinely and literally asked about an obscure word or passage, it should not be in any spirit of superiority. ("Even *I* can't understand it," is a rider often heard in the cloisters and quadrangles of the Daily Mirror.) If any line of the paper cannot be understood, it is not because of the limited education or intelligence of the reader but because of the limited ability or effort of the writer.

But "Will our readers living in Wigan understand this?" may as often as not be translated as, "Will newspapermen living in Petts Wood appreciate this?" The matter is frequently one of editorial taste and judgment — or what the questioner supposes editorial taste and judgment ought to be — rather than of clarity.

It should never be assumed, as the only yardstick, that any topic is outside the spectrum of interest of Mirror readers. Popular journalism was founded on the belief that ordinary people have an unquenchable thirst for information of all kinds. When the range of a typical saloon-bar discussion is more limited than that of the Mirror's usual editorial content (it never is) Northcliffe will have been proved wrong at last.

This is not to say that the Mirror is in the market for 2,000-word articles on porcelain. Its content is largely governed by its style, and its style is that of a tabloid newspaper, not of a learned journal. This extract from a front-page manifesto by Silvester Bolam (Editor 1948 — 1953) is still the best summary of what the Mirror is about:

> **The Mirror is a sensational newspaper. We make no apology for that. We believe in the sensational presentation of news and views, especially important news and views, as a necessary and valuable public service in these days of mass readership and democratic responsibility.**
>
> **We shall go on being sensational to the best of our ability...**
>
> **Sensationalism does not mean distorting the truth. It means the**

vivid and dramatic presentation of events so as to give them a forceful impact on the mind of the reader. It means big headlines, vigorous writing, simplification into familiar everyday language, and the wide use of illustration by cartoon and photograph...

Every great problem facing us — the world economic crisis, diminishing food supplies, the population puzzle, the Iron Curtain and a host of others — will only be understood by the ordinary man busy with his daily tasks if he is hit hard and hit often with the facts...

As in larger, so in smaller and more personal affairs, the Mirror and its millions of readers prefer the vivid to the dull and the vigorous to the timid.

No doubt we make mistakes, but we are at least alive.

Readers living in Wigan — and elsewhere — would still approve of that philosophy.

Over and under

None of the words italicised is necessary:

Pronounced there was more to come *later*
Razed *to the ground*
Battle lines are being drawn *up*
Shunted *off* **into the sidings**
Filled *up*
Said he had nothing *further* **to add to his statement**

Redundant words merely clutter the page, as do unnecessary auxiliaries and conjunctions *(he said he was* is as clear as *he said that he was)*. But beware of pruning too zealously. The following is from the Evening News, but it is the kind of over-cut writing that appears everywhere:

> The summary sacking in Haringey of three governors of a comprehensive school is a bizarre example of the new morality. During the caretakers' strike this winter the three did not want to keep the entire school open — merely to make sure that children nearing exams got tuition.

Had the passage read " — *they* merely *wanted* to make sure etc" it would not have been ambiguous.

Paragraphs

Fowler wrote that the purpose of paragraphing is to give the reader a rest.

Had he been more of a student of the popular Press he might have added that it is not the purpose of paragraphing to give the reader a jolt. That, however, is often the result.

Here is the intro of a feature on a visit by Elton John to Leningrad, as it appeared in print:

> **Russia is in the throes of a new revolution... thanks to rock superstar Elton John. Of course the fans have heard the music before.**

The two sentences seem contradictory. If the reader takes up Fowler's suggestion of a rest at the end of that paragraph, it can only be because he needs time to work out what these apparent non sequiturs add up to.

The story continues in paragraphs two and three:

> **Expensive cassettes recorded from black market albums or from crackling, distorted broadcasts by the BBC World Service circulate among young people.**
> **But until now they haven't had the chance of seeing the phenomenon of a live rock concert.**

All becomes clear — but in retrospect. The first sentence of the first paragraph ("Russia is in the throes of a new revolution... thanks to rock superstar Elton John") was meant to stand on its own. Either because that intro was deemed too short (See IMAGINARY RULES) or it didn't fit in with the page scheme, what should have been the opening sentence of the second paragraph was hooked on to it.

Had the paragraphing not been tinkered with, it would have fulfilled Fowler's other requirement: "The paragraph is essentially a unit of thought, not of length; it must be homogeneous in subject-matter and sequential in treatment."

Another example (one of very many) of the paragaph arrangement working against the text:

> **The Prince Regent, "Prinny", was a crazy punter. He had a runner that started hot favourite for the Derby and came in last.**
> **The horse ran again next day — unfancied — and won at a big price. The jockey got into serious trouble and was warned off. But Prinny later gave him a pension — which makes you wonder. King William IV was more interested in ships, so when his trainer asked him which of three horses he wished to be entered in a race in Derby week, he replied: "Send the whole fleet."**

Some readers (perhaps OUR READERS IN WIGAN, qv) might conclude that the Prince Regent and William IV were one and the same, and wonder not only why he gave the jockey a pension but how ships got into the story.

Even non-historians in newspaper offices will guess that there is a disguised "widow" in that baffling second paragraph. The story turned into a new leg on the second half of the word "wonder" — which should have ended a paragraph. To avoid leaving the syllable "— der" hanging on a top line (see IMAGINARY RULES again — or better still, do some re-jigging so that the problem doesn't occur), the stray syllable was hitched to the nearest paragraph.

To sum up:

Paragraphs should make the story easier to read, not harder.

And a final word from Fowler:

"There can be no general rule about the most suitable length for a paragraph; a succession of very short ones is as irritating as very long ones are wearisome."

Person to person

If the story involves the reader, then involve the reader. Use the second person, not the third person.

This makes a dull event even duller:

> **Everyone who makes his or her cross on a Euro-ballot paper on Thursday will be making a mark in history.**

It would have been livelier (and less clumsy) to have begun: "When you make your cross..."

Possessions

A BBC news-reader was recently heard to announce that a detective had flown from Singapore's Raffles Hotel to London's Heathrow to continue inquiries in London's Mayfair.

The possessive gazetteer — *Birmingham's New Street, Liverpool's Mersey, Brighton's West Pier, Cornwall's St. Ives* etc. — is now in use everywhere, except in the everyday English used by the Mirror's 12,000,000 readers.

Although it has no purpose and doesn't save space *Birmingham's New Street* is in fact one en *longer* than *New Street, Birmingham)* it is harmless enough — as is a nervous tic.

Puns and wordplay

On June 17 1952, the following thought from Lord Beaverbrook was conveyed to the staff of the Daily Express via their editorial bulletin:

" 'Once Britten twice shy' is a pun that will amuse some people and irritate others. We should rigorously, vigorously ban puns in headlines and text."

It was one more Beaverbrook cause that was doomed to failure. Today not only the Daily Express but all the national newspapers — and the provincial newspapers that emulate the national newspapers, and the small-town evenings that emulate the provincial papers, and the bright web-offset weeklies that emulate the small-town evenings — could be mistaken for Joe Miller's Joke Book.

What is remarkable about the following story?

BY GUM! THOSE BOOKIES FACED
A STICKY PROBLEM

One hundred London bookmakers faced a sticky situation when a quick-drying "superglue" was used to seal their front doors, it was disclosed yesterday.

Last night they were adhering to a theory that it could have been Scottish football fans on their way to Wembley who had gummed up the works last Saturday...

The remarkable thing is not that the story contains five puns in 61 words. That is about par for the course. The remarkable thing is that the story appeared in the Daily Telegraph. Ten years ago, a Telegraph man turning in such stuff would have been given sick leave.

The Telegraph missed the point, made in the Mirror, that the sticky campaign gave the bookies a right old pasting. But then the Mirror has always been the leader in this field. At a time when other papers were injecting puns and double entendres only into the occasional headline, as complained about by Beaverbrook, the Mirror's punsters were already making forays into the text.

As long ago as June 1939, the Mirror had this intro:

The writing on the wall is plain — the Welsh language must either adapt itself to its modern environment or perish, says the Welsh Department...

Forty years later, in June 1979, the Mirror was reporting:

The writing's on the wall for FBI fingerprint experts...

The paper that was forty years before its time (or forty years after its time, depending on how you look at it) with the writing-on-the-wall joke, can claim some other notable firsts.

It was the first paper to call women police officers *fair cops*. (The joke is still wheeled out once a year on what is probably its anniversary. Its latest appearance was on April 24 1979 when an account of "a stunning blonde model" detaining three car thieves went on to relate how "the story of the fair cop was told yesterday to Sunderland magistrates.")

It was the first paper to use the adjective *Purrfect* in connection with cats, and to begin cat stories with *Here is the mews*. It imported the American expression *in the doghouse* for extensive use in other pet stories.

It was the first paper to use the headline TEACHERS CANED, and may even be the last paper to use it, since this venerable gag shows no sign of being taken out of service. (The old headline has, indeed, been thoroughly overhauled and modernised and now regularly appears as SIR CANED.)

It was the first paper to use the caption intro *Eye eye!* when what were then called pin-ups had a nautical theme. It was, at the dawn of the permissive society, the first paper to describe two other pin-ups (by then known as Page Three girls) as *bosom pals*.

But those were the heady pioneer days. How is the Mirror placed in the punning race in a more sophisticated era when the new technology can inject up to twenty-five puns into a column of type without any human being having to use his hands or even his head? Here is a selection of recent efforts, with the puns italicised as they used to be in the Victorian comic papers where many of them first saw the light:

Waiter Charles Allcorn caused panic *by the plateful* at a smart seaside restaurant, it was claimed yesterday. One night he was said to have sprayed furniture polish over the cheese.

And that was only for *starters*...

CHIPPY GETS A *BATTERING*

The fat was in the fire when fish and chip shop owner John Rose fancied cod and chips on his night off.

He claimed his portion of cod was just warmed up. A row started... and Rose began *battering* the other chippy, Roger Thompson.

Flying tonite: First, he hurled a jar of vinegar...

A loving mum may find she's been *left holding the baby* after the birth of her first child.

MAL'S ROAD TO *HITCHES*

Hitch hiker Malcolm Skyner's holiday was full of *hitches*.

He thumbed it through America and Mexico — and it was *thumbs down* all the way...

Bus conductor Mark Pollock was left *holding tight* yesterday.

And he wasn't the slightest bit pleased about it.

For Mark was in a real *fix*... stuck fast to a handrail with Superglue...

A London Transport spokesman said it was the second time a conductor had been superglued by pranksters. The first victim stood in a layer of the stuff spread on the floor.

And just like Mark, he found himself *stuck in a solid jam.*

There must be something about the qualities of superglue that spurs the punster on to wilder and wilder efforts. Note that the item just quoted starts with the conventional superglue puns; but at the end of the story, the final glue pun is grafted on to a totally unexpected, and entirely unexplained, traffic jam pun. This is wordplay of truly Joyceian complexity.

GYMSHOE MAN GETS THE *BOOT*

Keep-fit enthusiast Bob Norburn got off *on the wrong foot* when he decided to jog to work...

Here we have a curiosity. *Boot* in the headline and *wrong foot* in the intro suggest that the punster is at work. But where is the subject of his pun? *Gymshoe man* might be it, but what on earth is a gymshoe man? Is it a strained synonym for *keep-fit enthusiast*, introduced to justify the *boot* and *wrong foot* jokes (not to mention the even better joke later on, when Mr. Norburn is reported to be *taking steps* to sue somebody)?

If we read on, all is revealed:

> **His foreman took one look at Bob's blue and white training shoes and told him to go home and change them.**

It now dawns on us that what we have here is an example of wordplay *(boot, wrong foot)* being introduced *before* the word that is being played on *(shoes)*. This is another innovation, worthy of the mind of a crossword compiler.

There is still room, however, for the old-fashioned, groan-inducing, really terrible pun as immortalised by Mr. Pooter in *The Diary of a Nobody* ("I'm 'fraid this shirt is *frayed!*").

> **TEDDY BEAR HUNTING IS NO *PICNIC***
> **A hunt for old teddy bears has proved *no picnic* for junk dealer Paul Burns.**
> **An American businessman wants to buy all the teds he can find — provided they are the older straw-stuffed variety.**
> **But so far Paul's had *barely* no success.**

Alas, the hilarious effect of *barely* is spoiled by its reducing the sentence in which it has been inserted to gibberish. (One negative cannot qualify another — even when one of them is a dreadful pun.)

The heights of punning and wordplay are reached in captions, and CAPTIONS are dealt with elsewhere. But perhaps the following may be borrowed from that category to show what gigantic strides the art has made since those primitive days of *Eye eye* and *Bosom pals:*

> **WHAT A *CORKER!***
> **Success is *brewing* for Pam Heaney. The 18-year-old who makes her own wine is having a *very good year* modelling. Her *intoxicating* looks are taking her all over the world. And *connoisseurs* agree that she *travels* beautifully.**

Truly the pun, like Miss Heaney, has travelled far — and with any luck it may travel farther yet.

All these examples may convey the flavour of puns as they appear in popular (and sometimes not so popular) newspapers, but it is difficult to convey their cumulative effect. What has to be remembered is that these are not stray puns or isolated puns or occasional puns, but that they appear *every* day on practically *every* page of *every* tabloid paper. On one entirely typical day, for instance, Mirror readers were able to learn within the space of three or four pages that builder George Lamb didn't turn up in court because he had suffered a real roasting, that Mary Poppins won't be popping out as a sexy siren just yet, that a multi-million-pound Dickens fantasy world for London is a Dickens of a good idea, that actor Andrew Ray found playing the part of a chain-smoker a choker, that pub landlady Iris Kirkman felt really tight and got all bottled-up after her wedge slippers tripped her up and she became wedged between two walls, and that pigeon fancier Dave Wareham, who appeared in court, had his wings clipped by the beak.

There will always be room for a really good pun or ingenious play on words in a headline, which is where the pun started its long and mainly undistinguished career in journalism (see ONE MORE TIME). There is hardly any place for it in the text. In either case, the story has to be of a very particular type to warrant tricks with words, and the tricks have to be brilliant and original ones. Automatic punning is a tedious schoolboy game which must leave the reader feeling as he would if he switched on his TV set and found Anna Ford playing ping-pong while reading the News at Ten.

The case against puns is the same as the case against FACETIOUSNESS (qv). There is one more point to be made.

On June 14 1979, a reader turned to page seven of his Daily Mirror and caught the words GRAVE AGONY in a headline. So conditioned was he by puns, double entendres and giggling innuendoes in his regular newspaper that a thin, anticipatory smile played on his lips as he rehearsed the comic-postcard possibilities of *grave*. The full headline, A TRAGIC MUM'S GRAVE AGONY, told him that the story was not meant to be funny after all.

Quote unquote

Except where obligatorily wrapped around passages of reported speech or introduced as typographical crossed fingers to ward off libel actions, inverted commas are haphazardly used in the Daily Mirror.

A piece about currency exchange controls says that they cost a fortune to *"police"* (in quotes) and that they *strangle* (not in quotes) business.

There is inconsistency here. The first word is in quotes because we don't mean *police* literally (or we think we don't, but the Concise Oxford gives "v.t… control"). But we don't mean *strangle* literally, either. So we should say either:

> **They cost a fortune to "police." They "strangle" business.**

or:

> **They cost a fortune to police. They strangle business.**

As always, the least fussy version is best.

Here is an example of quotes being used for all sorts of different reasons — not all of them completely justified:

> **Doctors have been given the go-ahead to prescribe a controversial "morning after" Pill.**
> **It is not foolproof, and it is to be used only as an "emergency measure" — for instance, to prevent a rape victim becoming pregnant…**
> **But it MIGHT NOT WORK, warns the Department of Health.**
> **And, if it fails, an embryo baby could be deformed.**
> **The "green light" for the method is given in the latest edition of the Health Department's handbook on birth control…**

Morning after seems to have been given quotes here because the (usually hyphenated) expression *morning-after Pill* is not yet deemed to be in general use.

It is not clear why *emergency measure* is in quotes. It is not an unusual phrase or saying. The words are not being used ironically.

No-one is being quoted (or perhaps they are? But the paragraph doesn't credit the source).

Green light is presumably in quotes because it is an expression borrowed from popular usage — slang, almost. But the newspapers are full of examples of everyday language (or if they are not, they should be). If they were to put them all in inverted commas, their pages would look like flypapers.

In the one place where quotation marks might have strengthened the story — on the warning from the Department of Health — they are not used, although even if the quote is indirect speech or a summary, they would have been justified. But at least this particular paragraph follows what should be a general principle:

Inverted commas clutter up the narrow columns of newspapers and should be used as little as possible.

Rank and file

In the armed forces, other ranks are often identified by their trade or calling — Rifleman Jones, Cook-corporal Smith, Signalman Brown, Telegraphist Black. Even Boy Robinson.

The practice has been adopted with gusto in Fleet Street.

On one single (and typical) day, the following roll-call could have been taken in the Daily Mirror lines:

American pro football star Bob Kuenchenberg
Australian champion Eddie Charlton
Author Daniel Defoe ("Creator of Robinson Crusoe")
Comedian Eric Sykes
Comedian Frankie Howerd

Charlie's Angel Cheryl Ladd
Chairman Harry Marshall
Darts lover and poet Betty Porter
Devoted family man Laurence Starn
Deputy assistant commissioner Peter Nevisen
Disgraced President Richard Nixon
Engineering President Terry Duffy
Father-of-four Abdul Shukur
Fifty-two-stone housewife Muriel Hopkins
Fly-half Dave Sorrell
Former Premier Michel Debre
Former world champion John Conteh
Football internationals and later managers
    Jimmy Dickinson and Tommy Docherty
Frenchman Jacques Morali
Goalkeeper Ray Clemence
Goalkeeper Dave Laurence
Gun-totin' dude Tex Tracey
Hotel manager John Lance
Instructor Ken Russell
Internationals Peter Barnes and Aša Hertford
Liberal leader David Steel
Love-tangle vicar Kenneth Flenley
Manager Brian Clough
Manager John Barnwell (and Assistant Richie Barker)
Manchester City manager Tony Book
Model Peta Seccombe
Mother-of-four Betty Akin
Novelist Anthony Trollope

Owner John Hayter
Policewoman Karen Fletcher
Polo-playing city gent Sandy Harper
Rolling Stone Keith Richards
Swansea Manager John Toshack
Security man Daniel Taylor
Stunning model Christian Arnott
Schoolboy Biff Smith
Schoolboy Richard Cuthbert
Schoolgirl Julie Beard
Social worker Eamonn Duffy
Super-scrounger Neimat Zafar
Teenager David Lear
Teenager John Dillon
Top Judge Lord Denning
Trainer George Francis
Trainer Duncan Sasse
Top Rank TV boss Bob Arum
Uganda dictator Idi Amin
Waitress Susan Kearly
Wealthy shipyard boss Christopher Bailey
Young England player Martin Beaver
Young soccer star Salvatore Bagni

Walking-on parts such as Premiers, Chancellors, Ministers and Shadow Spokesmen have been omitted from the above list for reasons of space. Several colourful characters — notably Watford rock star chairman Elton John, crafty cockney Eric Bristow, pint-sized heart-throb Ricky Shroder, fiery show-jumper Harvey Smith, and South West Water Authority information officer Peter Muggeridge — were regrettably absent in adjacent issues of the paper.

While there can be nothing in principle against the practice of prefacing names with potted biographies, sometimes it is difficult to see what is the principle that is being followed. How is it decided that, on the same page, Delhi science student Kapil Dev should appear as *Kapil Dev, a science student from Delhi,* while in the report of a Gillette Cup match between Lancashire and "Championship leaders Essex," Frank Hayes, who was far from fit, should appear as *far-from-fit Frank Hayes?*

This is one of those cases where an accepted convention becomes tedious and irritating when overdone. The above cast-list from one day's paper shows that it *is* overdone.

(See also ADJECTIVES)

Readers write

It's well known that over the years readers who write to the papers have evolved their own repertoire of tired phrases — "why oh why," "mere housewife," "was my face red" etc.

But do readers really refer to George Best as "the former Manchester United problem player"?

They do in the Daily Mirror.

Readers' letters should read like readers' letters. They should not reveal signs of heavy editorial compression or re-working (usually most evident in the obligatory summary of the topic under discussion: "I'm amazed at reader Mrs. I. Horler's narrow-minded view that motor sports should be banned until fuel supplies pick up again...").

On the other hand, they should not contain the kind of home-grown hackneyed expressions quoted above. Nor should they be a sanctuary for awkward English:

How unfortunate to have so little sense of humour as the recent reader who saw nothing to laugh at in ITV's "In Loving Memory."

A recent reader is a reader who is not long past. The Mirror prefers to have its readers living in the present.

Says who?

The place for the passive voice is Whitehall, not Fleet Street.

> **It is thought that Wednesday's Derby at Epsom could be the last to be shown by the BBC.**

It is thought by whom?

> **LWT are said to be particularly pleased with the Derby contract...**

Who said it?

The active voice is preferable for newspapers because it answers questions. The passive voice often sounds as if it had something to hide. It can also waste time:

> **Petrol is running out and booze is being put into fuel tanks.**

By whom? By Brazilians, it says in the second paragraph. Then why not say it in the first paragraph? Answer: because of the national newspaper principle that what happened is more interesting than where it happened. But is the principle infallible? The second paragraph reads:

> **So desperate is the world oil crisis that in Brazil they are putting alcohol in their cars.**

This repeats all the information we've just been given in the first paragraph, but makes a livelier job of it because the story now involves people.

The active voice is best even if the source has to be anonymous or general ("Police think" for "It is thought", "Officials believe" for "It is believed that"). If the source is the cuttings library, then the less said about what is said to have been said, the better.

Exception: "....it was claimed yesterday" in court story intros. This shorthand saves words and keeps the paper out of trouble.

Screamers

Exclamation marks should be used in exclamatory headlines (HAMMERED!), in reported speech ("Was my face red!"), in titles of films etc. ("Oliver!"), in editorial interjections ("Good God!") or exclamations ("Poppycock!") and as little as possible elsewhere.

The exclamation mark is an aid to good English. It is not a prop for bad writing.

A sentence that falls flat without an exclamation mark is a flat sentence. The exclamation mark will not inject drama into it. It must be re-cast.

An exclamation mark cannot tell the reader that a particular passage is funny. The most it can tell him is that it was meant to be funny.

Stagger off

Sums of money, percentages, weights, heights, depths, lengths, numbers, measurements by volume, temperatures, distances, prices, and so on, do not stagger.

Where *staggering* (going unsteadily as if about to fall; shaking conviction; giddiness as in horses and cattle disease) is supposed to convey *astonishing,* it no longer does. The word is worn out.

Supernumeraries

Super as a prefix still has plenty of tread left in it — *Superbrat,* for example, was original and evocative. But *superstar,* as applied to anyone who has made a couple of films or cut a couple of records, is surely played out by now. And there have been far too many *supermums* and *superdads* in the Daily Mirror.

Tabloidese

Tabloidese, that tough-guy, hat-on-the-back-of-the-head talk that makes the newspapers sound like James Cagney (RAP, PROBE, BID, SWOOP, AXE) was devised to accommodate the largest type to the smallest page.

Partly inspired by the back-numbers department of the New York Daily News (a newspaper which still uses a squeeze-bulb plate camera as its logo) and by old Death Row movies, it is essentially a made-up language, a kind of primitive Esperanto where nouns, verbs and adjectives are interchangeable. So long as readers are well-versed in this Esperanto, it is a useful — indeed an essential — headline aid. But is it always comprehensible? Do those who habitually ask, "Will our readers in Wigan understand this?" ever ask if Wigan readers can follow, for instance:

JAIL THREAT TO DRUG ROW STONE

That headline (from The Sun) is made up of five nouns and one preposition. At least one reader, grasping at straws, seized on *to* and thought he had found a verb: *to drug.* From this he concluded that there was a jail threat, i.e. a threat by the jail, to drug a row Stone. What was a row Stone? Presumably a Rolling Stone involved in a row. Very well: a jail threatens to drug (with tranquillisers?) a Rolling Stone either involved in a quarrel or making a noise.

The text suggests a different interpretation: A Rolling Stone, Keith Richards *(Stone)* was given what the Canadian Justice Department believes to be a lenient suspended sentence for a drug offence *(drug row)* and they want him put in prison *(jail threat).*

Having worked that out, the reader from Wigan (or the Bronx) may now pit his wits against this Mirror headline:

TORCH BOY SET ABLAZE BY GANG

Set ablaze by gang is clear enough, but what is a *torch boy*? It can only be (see story) a boy who has been set ablaze. So if the Esperanto headline were translated into something approaching English, it would read:

ABLAZE BOY SET ABLAZE BY GANG

Is the headline TRIPLE LOVE-SNATCH BOY IS HUNTED any relation to TORMENT OF A LOVE-TUG MUM? Do we all understand, without reference to the story, that a *triple love-snatch boy* is one who has been seized by his father, from his mother, for the third time? Do we have some idea what a *love-tug mum* is? If so, does it confuse us or enlighten us when in the first paragraph of the accompanying story she becomes a *love-tug wife?*

Until present trends are reversed and tabloids start going broadsheet, there will always be a demand for short bold words to fit big bold headlines. There is no reason why these should not be "label" words, found nowhere else in the language — a label, after all, is precisely what the headline is. But as any reputable patent medicine manufacturer would agree, a label must tell the consumer clearly what is in the bottle. If it doesn't, it is a case of either quackery, flimflam or incompetence.

But what of tabloidese "label" words that — seemingly with the same territorial ambitions as PUNS — have slunk down from the headline to the text? What are they doing there? The average news story, after all, is not set in 144 point. True, space is always at a premium, but is it at such a premium that the reader must have his Esperanto dictionary at the ready?

Doctors and ambulancemen were *slammed* **yesterday....**

Diesel train services are to be *axed* **by British Rail in a desperate** *bid* **to save fuel...**

A lonely old peer lured young girls into bed for *sex romps...*

A *call* **for Britain to take in more Vietnamese boat people was made yesterday...**

A *blaze superstore* **has told its** *till girls,* **"Dump the money and run for your lives"**...

It could be argued that most of these words have been used (overused?) so often that readers know exactly what they mean. Probably so, in the headline sense. But what, outside the headlines, is a *sex romp?* What is a *blaze superstore?* Who are *till girls?* Why, if these words are now so common, are they not in common use? Why do we not hear housewives at bus-stops saying "Our Marlene used to be a till-girl at that blaze superstore" or "Did I tell you about young Fred being rapped after he slammed his boss? He thinks he's going to be axed"? Words that have never managed to get into the mainstream of the language are suspect as a means of popular communication.

They are, and remain, labels. They do not convey precise meanings. The reader looks at the label, opens the tin — and finds a tin of labels.

Tabloidese is essentially *passive.* In tabloid-land, *400 jobs face axe.* In real life, 400 men may lose their jobs. Intended to be dramatic, tabloidese has a curiously deadening effect. *A pay war loomed last night* is not dramatic because it has all the ingredients of drama except the players — the story does not come to life until we know who is involved in it.

Tired quotes

Some of the best writing in the Daily Mirror is to be found between inverted commas. Perhaps we interview a more interesting class of people than other papers — at any rate, we get the better quotes, with the true flavour of doorstep English. (As an example of a newspaper with a tin ear, see the San Francisco Chronicle which carried this alleged quote from an English couple in a story about a ferry strike: "This is a lousy break for us, because we're here from England and we were told the ferry was a great treat. It's just too bad because we're headed for Los Angeles this afternoon and I guess we won't have a chance to ride the boat.")

But the public, like the Press, has an extensive repertoire of phrases that have seen better days: *It was like Aladdin's cave in there... I'm over the moon... worse than the Blitz... they were like animals... sick as a parrot... not good enough... driving like maniacs... winter of discontent... I was sickened... never had a chance... saw this ball of fire coming towards us...*

Stereotyped talking is to be avoided as much as stereotyped writing.

The tops

Top, as meaning senior, highly-placed, important etc., is a lazy word that does not earn its keep. Its purpose often seems to be to impress the reader rather than to inform him.

Compare the degrees of topness of the following *top* people or institutions:

> **Top disc-jockey Tony Blackburn**
> **A top firm** (i.e., the Wm. Press civil engineering company)
> **A top judge** (a U.S. Federal judge)
> **Spain's top pop star**
> **Top people's store Harrods**
> **One top stockbroker-economist**
> **Top judge Lord Denning** (who, incidentally, is reported to have got a wigging)
> **Three top Spanish matadors**
> **Top producer Dr Jonathan Miller**

All these appeared in a top national newspaper, the Daily Mirror, within a day or two of one another. The description *top* is in some of these cases unnecessary, in others of doubtful suitability, and in yet others so vague as to be without any meaning.

Top reached its peak in a short report about a week of British TV programmes in Los Angeles:

> **Thames Television today takes over the peak viewing of a top Los Angeles TV channel for a week.**

Readers were left to work out for themselves what a *top* TV channel might be. If they read other papers — which reported that the British programmes were not carried by any of the three major network channels — they might have concluded that a top Los Angeles TV channel is one where programmes are not dubbed into Spanish.

Top has become a reflex word. It has not been helped by the legions of top models who have graced the Mirror's pages (it is odd that the punsters have not discovered any bottom models). It is too all-embracing to be accurate, and should be discouraged.

The weather-vane

Extremes of weather (i.e., when Britain sizzles or the BRRometer is below freezing point) always provide a good opportunity to test prevailing facetiousness levels.

The following reading, taken during a heatwave in the period under review, shows puns and wordplay at dangerously near the contamination mark:

COOL IT! IT'S A BLOWN PHEWS
Britain was on the boil again yesterday — but don't presume we're going to get into the hotspot habit.
For weathermen warned that the phews has failed...

The previous day's weather headline —

Return of the PHEW!

— had the merit of being less groan-inducing, but was let down by the intro, which had June bustin' out all over (song-title: 1954) yet again. But it is interesting that all the PHEW variations, whether weak or witty (usually weak) depend for their effect on the reader's recollection of the greatest headline cliche of all time. PHEW! WHAT A SCORCHER! was worn so threadbare in its day that any reference to it is supposed to be a shared joke between newspaper and reader — a rare case of a trade choosing to remind the customers of its own shoddy workmanship.

The PHEW joke has been so overdone that it has become a cliché born of a cliché.

To return to weather stories in general:

They have always attracted a determinedly boisterous approach, partly because the British weather is commonly a subject for saloon-bar jocularity and partly because since only unusual weather is worth reporting, the round-up tends to be larger than life. (An excellent example appears under AND.)

Temperatures *soar* (or *plunge*), Britain *swelters (or shivers)* — and *there's more to come, say the weathermen* (or: *But make the most of it, say the weathermen).* Allowing that it's the same story every year, this year's story does not necessarily have to read like a photocopy of last year's story.

What ho and all that rot

National newspapers intending to flourish in the nineteen-eighties should not use expressions that belong to the eighteen-nineties.

But they do.

Royal Ascot stories ("THE BOUNDER WHO BARGED THE QUEEN. He may have looked like a toff in his top hat and tails. But, by George, the man was a cad.") and public school stories ("I say, you chaps! Here's some jolly frightful news about Eton.") must make readers wonder whether they are reading a modern daily paper or a back number of The Magnet (expired 1940).

P. G. Wodehouse and Frank Richards, both past their prime when their idiosyncratic prose first came to be commonly imitated in Fleet Street, and both long since dead, never pretended that they were reproducing real-life speech patterns. Richards borrowed from Kipling's *Stalky & Co* (1899) and Wodehouse took many of his "man-about-town" expressions from W. S. Gilbert (born 1836).

The following expressions survive in reprinted editions of the dead authors mentioned, and in the news columns of contemporary popular newspapers:

All, dash it	Frightful, jolly
Ass, prize	Gad, by
Aunt, giddy, my	George, by
Aunt, sainted, my	Gosh, golly
Beasts, those	Gumdrops, golly
Blighter	Haddocks, oh
Bounder	Ho, tally
Brigade, top-hat-and-spats	Ho, what
Cad	It, hang
Chappies, those Eton	Jape
Chaps, look here you	Jeeves, I say
Crikey	Jolly, awfully, how
Die, laugh my dear, I thought I'd	Jove, bai
Deuced	Know, doncher
Escutcheon, blot on the old	Lark, what a
Fellows, I say you	Lor', good

Nerve, what a bally
Pip, pip
Priceless
Really, oh
Rotters
Rot, what absolute
Shame, dashed
Show, bad
Sir, Gad

Spiffin'
Stars, oh my
Thick, I say chaps it's a bit
Toff
Whacko
What, eh
What, what
Wheeze, I say chaps here's a
Yaroo

Which is that?

Which and *that* are regularly confused, in the mistaken belief that they are always interchangeable.

An over-simple definition, which at any rate will serve to cover those areas of meaning where the confusion is most likely to be found, is:

That defines.

Which informs.

(*That* should be used without a comma. The clause introduced by *which* is usually contained within commas or preceded by one.)

The difference illustrated:

"The piece *that* the Editor jumped up and down on is in the wastepaper basket." This assumes that we already know about the Editor's impetuous reaction, which is mentioned only so that we will know what piece is being talked about when we are given the news about it being thrown into the wastepaper basket.

But:

"The piece, *which* the Editor jumped up and down on, is in the waste paper basket." This assumes that we already know which piece is being talked about, but we are being given *new information* about the Editor's jumping-up-and-down activities.

What is style?

This is Daily Mirror style:

> Almost all of Norman Scott's adult life has been dedicated to one purpose: to prove that his story about Jeremy Thorpe was true.
>
> Wherever the Liberal chief turned throughout the extraordinary saga, he was confronted by the brooding obsession of his accuser.
>
> For the past two years Scott has conducted his campaign from his isolated home near Chagford on the edge of Dartmoor. He makes his living schooling horses and giving dressage lessons.
>
> He has continued to insist that he is concerned only that the truth should come out.
>
> But his crusade has looked more and more like a vendetta against the man he blames for years of misery.
>
> Scott is thirty-nine. He was born Norman Valentine Josiffe, the son of working class parents at Bromley, Kent.
>
> After leaving school he went to work at stables in Oxfordshire owned by a friend of Thorpe. It was there that he first met the politician...

There is not a Thorpe trial every day but there is writing of that calibre somewhere in the Daily Mirror on most days. It is a plain, straightforward, well-ordered narrative, completely without gimmicks. There are no fancy words, and no needless words. The 150-word passage quoted contains only four adjectives, of which two convey information and the other two convey atmosphere. The material is arranged chronologically, with the briefest of introductions. No attempt is made to tempt the reader with window-dressing or with lurid shock-drama labels, yet he is gripped from the start.

Does this mean that the Mirror is at its best only when writing seriously about serious matters? Not at all. This too is Daily Mirror style:

> Bachelor Stephen Howe really has his hands full running his own home.
>
> He even turned down a free trip to the Continent because it would interfere with his housework.

The refusal angered his bosses, who had asked him to represent them at a scientific conference in Brussels.

Stephen, 29, said: "Spending time away from home creates a backlog of housework, gardening and laundry."

His bosses at Stone Platt Fluid Fire, Dudley, West Midlands, were amazed.

Company chairman Nathan Myers pointed out that Stephen was the only man capable of telling the conference about research he had been doing.

And Mr. Myers went out of his way to eliminate any fears Stephen might have about the trip.

Frightened of flying? he asked Stephen.

No problem. We'll send you by sea.

Reluctant to spend two days away from home?

No problem. We'll make it a one-day trip.

But Stephen was adamant, and came up with a string of other reasons for not going. Such as...

- I don't possess a decent suit.
- Foreign food upsets me.
- I haven't got a passport.
- I would have to buy a suitcase.

Eventually Mr. Myers got tough. Either you go to Brussels, he said — or you're fired.

Stephen, who owns a terraced house on a luxury estate in Wolverhampton, stuck to his guns.

He took Mr. Myers to a Birmingham industrial tribunal alleging wrongful dismissal.

And the judgment went against Stephen — the houseproud bachelor who polished off his job.

Apart from the *really* blemish in the intro (see OH, REALLY?), and the fall from grace in the last sentence where the lure of the pun becomes too strong, the report is free of the cloying facetiousness that usually coats this type of story like melted toffee. Again we have a story straightforwardly told. The humour of the tale emerges without digging the reader in the ribs. It is well-shaped. And for once italics, bold type and blobs are put to a constructive use: they help the narrative along, as well as eliminating an excessive clutter of quotation marks.

A last brief example (of many available). A picture of Frank Sinatra playing chess with (and losing to) the world champion Anatoly Karpov was a ripe opportunity for Ol' Blue Eyes jests or chess jokes, had the Mirror wanted to stay on the familiar tracks. Instead, the headline had Sinatra saying: NICE MOVE,

WISE GUY, NOW LET'S HEAR YOU SING. Not a pun in sight. That too is Daily Mirror style.

What is this style? Why do some stories, captions and headlines have it and others not? It would be fruitless to try to define it — as Fats Waller said when asked for a definition of jazz, "Lady, if you have to ask, I can't tell you." Obviously it demands flair, plus professionalism — two commodities that have never been in short supply in popular journalism. It demands experience, a quality that may be taken for granted at the Mirror. For the rest, it consists simply of choosing a handful of words from the half a million or so samples available, and arranging them in the best order. Neither this manual nor any other can show anyone how to do that, but for those who wish to be reminded of the ground-rules of what they now do by instinct, the following notes may be useful.

Use specific words *(red and blue)* not general ones *(brightly coloured)*.

Use concrete words *(rain, fog)* rather than abstract ones *(bad weather)*.

Use plain words *(began, said, end)* not college-educated ones *(commenced, stated, termination)*.

Use positive words *(he was poor)* not negative ones *(he was not rich* — the reader at once wants to know, how not rich was he?).

Use the active voice *(Police took no action)* not the passive voice *(No action was taken)*.

Don't overstate: *fell* is starker than *plunged*.

Don't lard the story with emotive or "dramatic" words *(astonishing, staggering, sensational, shock)*.

Avoid non-working words that cluster together like derelicts *(but for the fact that, the question as to whether, there is no doubt that)*.

Don't use words thoughtlessly. *(Waiting* ambulances don't rush victims to hospital. Waiting ambulances wait. Meteors fall, so there can be no *meteoric* rise.)

Don't use auxiliaries or conditionals *(was, might, would, should, may* etc) unless you have to. *(Mrs Thatcher is a political Florence Nightingale,* not *Mrs Thatcher* might be termed *a political Florence Nightingale.)*

Don't use unknown quantities (*very, really, truly, quite.* How much is *very?*).

Never qualify absolutes. A thing cannot be *quite impossible, glaringly obvious* or *most essential,* any more than it can be *absolutely absolute.*

Don't use wrong prepositions. (Check them for sense: we may *agree on* this point; you may *agree with* this opinion; he may *agree to* this proposal.)

Don't use jargon, clichés, puns, elegant or inelegant variations, or inexact synonyms (BRAVE WIFE DIED SAVING HER SON is wrong: wife is not a synonym for mother).

Use short sentences, but not all of the same length. A succession of one-clause sentences is monotonous and wearying.

Avoid elaborate construction. Take the sentence to pieces and recast it — probably as two sentences.

If a sentence reads as if it has something wrong with it, it has something wrong with it. *Whether you are motoring to see Mum, play trains in a railway museum or take in a stately home, this long Spring weekend can bring agony and death* is technically correct, but ugly.

Don't vary your rhythms for the sake of it. *He was not ill, and neither was he poor* is unnecessary variation. But there is a dramatic unity in *He was not ill. He was not poor.*

Even in a chronological narrative, the story should not start before it begins. *John Smith was really looking forward to his dinner* starts too early; the reader wants the dinner. Compare this with the opening of a short story by O Henry: *So I went to the doctor.* A whole paragraph has happened offstage, and the reader is plunged straight into the action.

Words are facts. Check them (spelling and meaning) as you would any other.

Unlike every manual on style ever prepared, this one has reached its last pages without quoting the King James Bible as an example of how English may be written at its best. The omission will now be put right, but indirectly.

In his 1946 essay, *Politics and the English Language,* George Orwell takes this passage from Ecclesiastes:

> I returned, and saw under the sun, that the race is not to the swift, nor the battle to the strong, neither yet bread to the wise, nor yet riches to men of understanding, nor yet favour to men of skill; but time and chance happeneth to them all.

He disembowels it, stuffs it with sawdust, and re-presents it as "officialese":

> Objective consideration of contemporary phenomena compels the conclusion that success or failure in competitive activities exhibits no tendency to be commensurate with innate capacity, but that a considerable element of the unpredictable must invariably be taken into account.

That is the kind of Whitehall gobbledygook that the Mirror has lampooned over the years. Yet how, forty years after Orwell's parody, would the same passage appear in a popular newspaper?

> Using your loaf won't fill your bread-bin, a mystery preacher warned in a pulpit blast yesterday.
> And punters will be pipped to know that though the horse they backed is first past the post — they won't pick up their winnings.
> HE-MEN have had it, according to the no-holds-barred sermon....

That's not style. But it's what gets into newspapers.